Fancywork and Fashion's

Time Machine:
The Modern Girls

by Joan Hinds and Jean Becker

Home movies, snapshots and vivid memories from the 1930s through the 1990s gave us our inspiration. Sometimes we can still hear the rustling of a can-can and feel the crispy, scratchy nylon and velvet confections we wore to birthday parties and recitals when we were children. A scrap of familiar fabric or an old pattern envelope can trigger memories of what was happening in the outside world while our mothers and grandmothers lovingly dressed us like little dolls. You have precious memories of your own. Join us while we reminisce; let us show you how to fit patterns to your doll collection and then create costumes that reflect our collective history.

Fancywork and Fashion Press
Duluth, Minnesota

Acknowledgements

Thanks to our customers who keep asking for more patterns; to Steve Tiggemann of Jeff Frey Photography & Associates, who laughs with us and not at us; to Götz Dolls, Inc. who authorized the use of their products in our photographs; to Sue Hartwig and Teri Monchamp of Rosebud Creations, who tried to teach us how to paint dolls, told us what kind of patterns dollmakers want, and loaned us dolls and props; to Julia Bly and Joan's mom Nina Sudor for lending us props; to our local Red Cross chapter for WWII posters; to our local library's collection of Ladies' Home Journal and McCall's Magazine through history; to Karen Cermak, our advisor and seamstress; and to Jean's mom, Selma, who saved every single pattern and doll garment she ever made for her daughter.

Credits

Götz Dolls appear with permission from their manufacturer, Götz Dolls, Inc. American Girls and Pleasant Company are registered trademarks of Pleasant Company. Rick Rack, Fray-Chek, Velcro, Simplicity and Betsy McCall are registered trademarks.

All porcelain dolls appearing in this book were made from the artists' molds and interpreted by various dollmakers.

ISBN 0-9636287-2-0

FANCYWORK and FASHION PRESS
4728 Dodge Street
Duluth, MN 55804

Introduction:

A Mystifying Array of Possibilities

As you look at the photos on the next two pages, you can probably see that not all so-called 18" dolls are created equal. Nor are the 16" or 20" ones. Some have long, slim legs. Others have short, chubby ones. Some dolls represent a 4-year-old's figure, others look like a 10 or 12-year-old. So some have pot bellies and others have waistlines. And those are just the porcelain, composition or hard plastic bodies.

Then there are the cloth-bodied dolls, and all bets are off with them. Some don't have shoulders, a proper butt or may bear very little resemblance to an actual human form even when they are made correctly! But face it, even if you are an accomplished dollmaker and have no trouble at all painting the porcelain head, arms and legs, how do you decipher the cloth body instructions? Aren't they sometimes vague and incomplete, lacking in helpful illustrations? Where are you supposed to attach the arms and legs? How much stuffing should you use? Try as you might, the "standard" body is difficult to achieve.

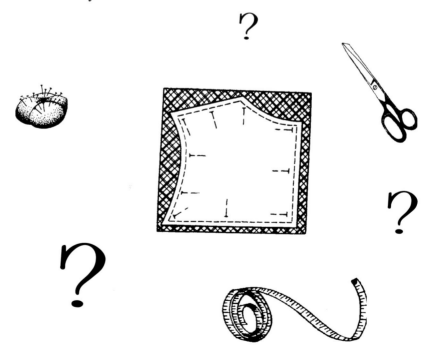

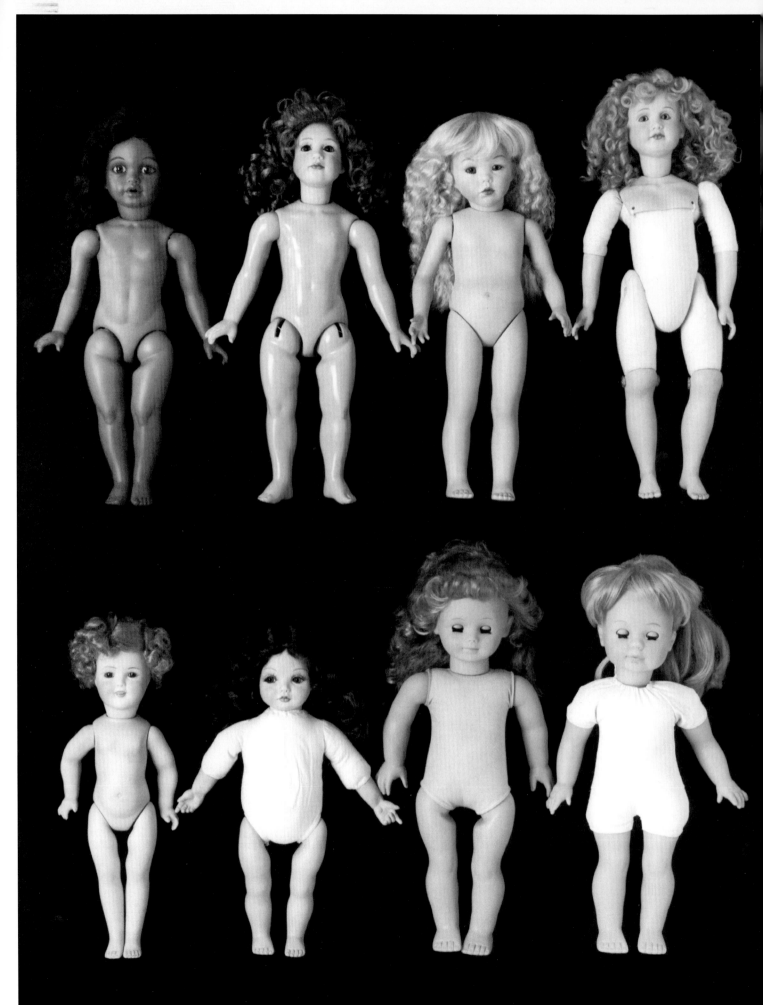

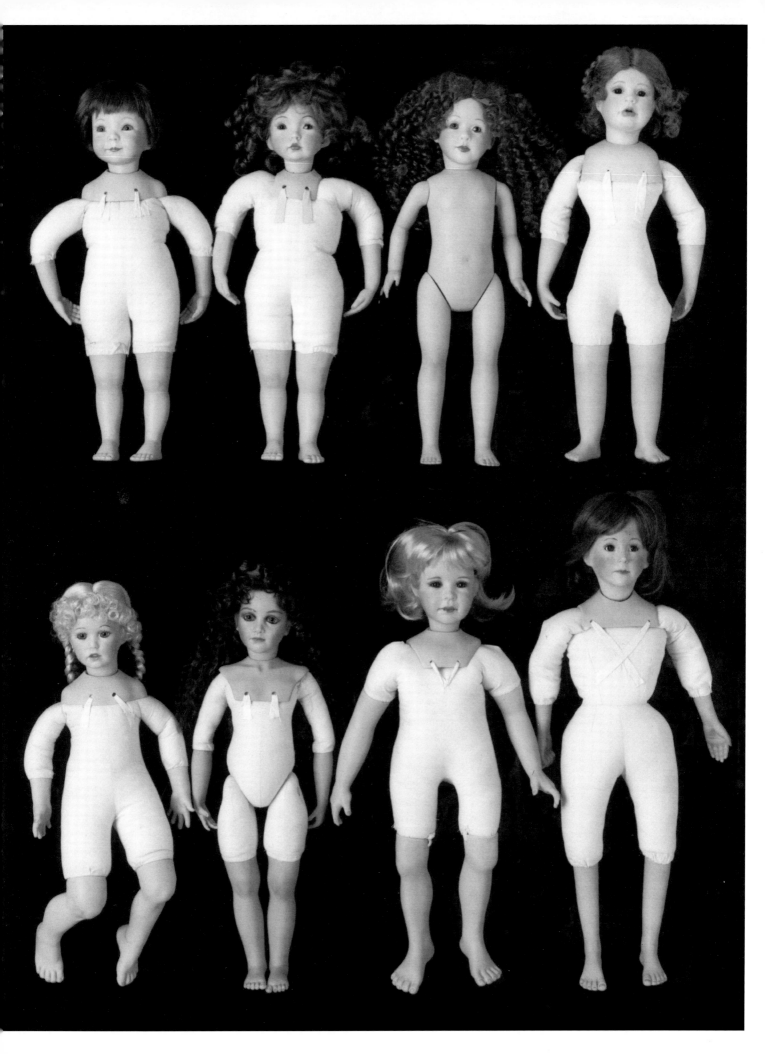

Who Are Those Naked Dolls, Anyway?!

Because we are frequently asked about the doll models we use in our books, we will identify them by doll's name, height, sculptor, company from which it can be ordered as of Fall 1994, and wig. We apologize if any of this information is incomplete or changes before the book reaches your hands. The doll industry is very dynamic, and sources come and go. Suppliers' addresses and phone numbers as we now know them are listed at the end of this book.

The porcelain faces were interpreted by various artists--some professional, some not.

Page 4, starting on the top row, going left to right:

"Angel," 18 inches, by C. Paul Jackson and Bunny Morris, Seeley's head mold, body from Seeley's mold ALB9873; shown here in Global's Zobe' wig, 10-11, dark brown. In the 1950's kitchen scene she appears in Monique's Cindy wig, 10-11, black.

"May," 18 inches, by Jane Zidjunas for Seeley's, on Seeley's 14" composition body MB140S; shown here in Global's Candi wig, 9-10, auburn. In the 1960's rec room scene she appears in Global's Carmen wig, 9-10, auburn.

"Hilary," 18 inches, by Dianna Effner for The Ultimate Collection, body from The Doll Artworks' T.J. 501 mold; shown here in Monique's pale blond long and wavy wig, 10-11. In the slumber party scene she appears in Expression's Heather wig, blond.

"Elise," 19 inches, by Jane Zidjunas for The Doll Carriage, cloth body from the pattern provided by the mold company; shown here in Monique's Erika, 10-11, light brown.

"Shirley," 16 inches, head unidentified (many Shirleys have been produced by many mold companies), body from Scioto's Character Body Mold 623; shown here in Playhouse's Shirley wig, size unknown, blond.

"Shy Violet," 16 inches, Klowns by Kay, cloth body from the pattern provided by the mold company; shown here in Playhouse's April wig, 10-11, dark brown.

Ginger," 18 inches, by Götz Dolls, 1991, vinyl on cloth body. Same body as that used on American Girls dolls by Pleasant Company. Wears the same size as "Anne" below.

"Anne," 18 inches, by Götz Dolls, 1994, vinyl on cloth body. Non-articulated arms and legs, but otherwise same body as that used on American Girls dolls by Pleasant Company. Identical body to "Hannah" in 1950's kitchen scene and "Pui Ling" in 1960's rec room scene.

Page 5, starting on the top row, going left to right:

"Bedtime Jenny" (often called "Smiling Jenny"), 19 inches, by Dianna Effner for Expressions, cloth body from the pattern provided by the mold company; shown here in Expressions' Jenny wig, brown.

"Emily," 19 inches, by Dianna Effner for Expressions, cloth body from the pattern provided by the mold company; shown here in Playhouse's Roma wig, 12-13, strawberry. In the 1950's schoolroom scene she appears in Wee Three's Ellen wig, 12-13, brown.

"Christina," 20 inches, by Astrid Essberger for The Doll Artworks, body from The Doll Artworks' T.J. 512 mold; shown here Global's Aerielle wig, 9-10, carrot.

"Tiffany," 20 inches, by Linda Mason for The Doll Artworks, cloth body from the pattern provided by the mold company; shown here in Wee Three's Ellen wig, 12-13, blond.

"Shay," 20-21 inches with bent legs, by Donna RuBert for The Doll Artworks, cloth body from the pattern provided by the mold company; shown here in Monique's Connie wig, 10-11, pale blond. In the 1950's schoolroom scene she appears in Global's mohair Sabine wig, 9-10, pale blond.

"Georgia," 21 inches, by Jane Zidjunas for The Doll Carriage, cloth body from the pattern provided by the mold company; shown here in Global's Dawnel wig, 10-11, auburn.

"Heidi," 22 inches, by Heidi Plusczok for Bell Ceramics, body from the pattern provided by the mold company; shown here in Playhouse's Debbie wig, 12-13, pale blond.

"Willow," 23 inches, by Dianna Effner for The Ultimate Collection, cloth body from the pattern provided by the mold company; shown here in Playhouse's Doris wig, brown. In the 1950's schoolroom scene she appears in Bell's Sissy wig, 11-12, auburn.

Chapter 1

A not-so-modern problem

On top of all the variables mentioned in the introduction is a major problem that's haunted doll owners for nearly a century: dollmakers attaching doll heads to a body other than the one originally intended by the sculptor. Yeah, you know what we're talking about. In antique price guides you will find mention of rare finds, hybrids of one style head and another style body. Sometimes the flesh tones don't even match. Maybe a valuable French head has been put on a sawdust-filled muslin body with crudely carved wooden hands and feet. Sometimes a manufacturer simply ran out of the correct parts and made substitutions. Clearly such an antique doll has an interesting history that can make it even more valuable than the standard.

But the proportions are a little peculiar. Your eye tells you something is not right, though you can't quite put your finger on it. Maybe the child doll has stubby toddler hands. Maybe the head is just too small or large in comparison to the torso. It's something....

And now the problem is even more rampant with modern porcelain dolls, and we who dabble in dollmaking sometimes contribute to the confusion. When each doll artist sculpts new arms and legs for each new head, porcelain shop owners are tempted to purchase only the head mold. Let's face it, the molds are pricey and if that particular doll proves not to be popular, the shop can be stuck with an expensive albatross. So they gamble that certainly some hands and feet mold they already own will work with the new head. Surely some cloth body pattern they already have photocopied 50 times will do the trick. Or if the customer wants, there's always a "similar" porcelain body mold already in stock. And anyway, some customers prefer a porcelain body when cloth is called for, and vice versa. The customer is always right, right?

So now you have a doll whose face looks like the one in the magazine ad and you should be able to purchase a pattern that claims to fit that particular named doll. But wait a minute, you're not buying a pattern for a head, you're buying a pattern for a body! Just whose body do you have anyway? (We're not happy with our bodies either, but that's another story.)

SOME OPTIONS

First, you may just get lucky. Maybe the doll you own is precisely as she was intended. And maybe the pattern you purchase not only is the perfect style you wanted but also fits like a dream. And the instructions are clear, there are lots of illustrations, and everything makes sense. (Boy, you really are lucky. Can we tag along when you go to buy lottery tickets?)

But if you're not so sure about what you've got, and you made the doll yourself, ask your porcelain doll instructor to identify the body you ended up using. If you purchased the doll and can't trace the source, take its measurements and compare them to our chart; pick the body type closest to your doll's.

There will be lots of possible variables, so keep in mind that the shoulder and waist measurements are the most critical for a good fit in our dress designs.

MEASUREMENTS OF OUR DOLLS

DOLL BODY	BACK (shoulder seam to shoulder seam)	WAIST (without stand)	BACK NECK TO FLOOR
Shirley (Scioto Character Body Mold 623)	4"	8"	12"
Shy Violet	5-1/2"	9-1/2"	12"
Götz/Pleasant Co. (vinyl with cloth)	5"	11"	13-1/2"
Hilary (T.J. 501)	4-1/2"	9"	14"
Christina (T.J. 512)	4-1-2"	9-1/2"	15"
Emily/Jenny	5"	12-1/2"	15"
Angel (Seeley ALB9873)	4-1/2"	9"	14"
May (Seeley MB140S)	4-1/2"	9-1/4"	14"
Elise	5"	10"	15-1/2"
Georgia	5"	10"	16-1/2"
Shay	5-1/2"	10-1/2"	8-1/2" to bottom of crotch
Tiffany	5-1/2"	10-1/4"	16-1/2"
Willow	5-1/2"	11"	19-1/2"
Heidi	5-1/2"	13-1/2"	17"

Once you have selected the closest body type, check the back-neck-to-floor measurement. Length is the easiest thing to adjust, so it's also easy to forget. Before cutting out sleeves and skirts, make sure you have made them long enough and allowed for cuffs, elastic and hems.

WHAT IF THESE BODICES AND SLEEVES ARE JUST NOT CLOSE ENOUGH?

We promise not to call this next part "tailoring" if you promise not to be afraid. Altering a given pattern piece is not difficult, honest! And remember, the style of dress most people make for child dolls--the waisted or yoke dress-- is very forgiving. It's not as though you have to deal with darts and shoulder pads and lapels. So take a deep breath and go get the paper towels.

That's right, paper towels. The ones that claim to be "just like cloth" work a lot better than the cheap, coarse ones, so spend 40 cents more. It's worth it when you try to stitch the pieces together. (Of course, you can use muslin or leftover fabric scraps or thin interfacing, but paper towels are always available and make great custom pattern pieces.)

Trace our bodice/yoke and sleeve pattern pieces closest to your doll's body type and size. If you're using white paper towels you might be able to trace from the pattern to the paper towel directly. If not, trace onto plain white paper, cut out the paper pieces and trace around them onto paper toweling. (You can see why working with thin interfacing, if you have it lying around, can be a step-saver.)

NEWSFLASH! All of our garment designs include enough "ease" (that's the roominess within the garment) to allow for an under-the-arms style stand. We like to conceal the stand if possible, plus costuming a doll that is already in a stand is just plain easier than working with one lying limply on a table. It frees up your hands and thus results in more accurate fit. So if you end up designing your own pattern pieces, or modifying ours, remember to leave room for the stand inside the dress.

1/4" SEAM ALLOWANCES ARE INCLUDED IN ALL PATTERN PIECES, so keep that in mind when laying the toweling pieces on the doll's body. If things look good, pin the bodice and sleeves together along seam lines as though you were completing a dress. You can even baste them together by machine and try the resulting paper bodice on to make sure the pattern works.

If some slight changes are needed, you can draw new necklines, new shoulder lines, or new armholes on the toweling pattern as it is worn by the doll and re-cut the adjustments, then proceed to check the fit. When everything looks good basted together, you know you have the right pattern pieces. Pull out the basting stitches and use the paper towel pieces, or trace them onto more durable paper and cut them out.

HINT: Use a different color of pattern paper for each doll. That way, when you find an orphan pattern piece six months down the road (of course, this never happens to us!), you know exactly in which doll's pattern envelope it belongs.

What you've just done is create a "sloper," a basic set of pattern pieces that you know fit your doll. Now comes the exciting part, where you get to be a creative designer. But first you should know some basics about style.

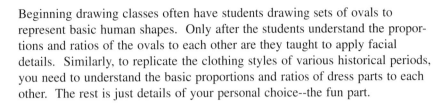

Chapter 2

Recognizing Your Era

Joan

Jean

Beginning drawing classes often have students drawing sets of ovals to represent basic human shapes. Only after the students understand the proportions and ratios of the ovals to each other are they taught to apply facial details. Similarly, to replicate the clothing styles of various historical periods, you need to understand the basic proportions and ratios of dress parts to each other. The rest is just details of your personal choice--the fun part.

Remember how your mother used to say that if she kept a dress long enough, it would eventually come back into style? Well, she was right. And the reason behind this is that a dress is a dress is a dress. It has some kind of bodice, some kind of sleeves, and some kind of skirt. What changes with history is the shape of these components, and to a lesser degree, their color. The probable combinations are mathematically limited, so you don't have to be more than middle-aged before the "new look from Paris" seems a little familiar.

The basic components of an era's style dress--the bodice, sleeves and skirt-- have a certain recognizable silhouette that identifies it and locks it into a historical time frame. We don't claim to be experts on exactly how long it takes for these things to cycle around, but we have noticed that the hottest back-to-school trend for the class of '94-95 is the mini baby doll dress. Well excuse us, but guess what we were wearing to junior high school in '64-65. And guess what hemlines were like for little girls in the '30s.

We started this book with the 1930's because we see that time period as truly "modern." That was an arbitrary decision due in large part to our being able to talk to our own mothers about that time period. Also, it seemed to us that there already were a lot of books in the library about doll costuming previous to that decade, and that anything afterwards fell into a new classification.

Silhouettes of the Great Depression

While the world slid inexorably toward a second global conflict, the 1930s ushered in great poverty for millions of Americans. Rural families fled their eroded, drought-ridden farms for the city, hoping for jobs. Urban unemployment led to soup kitchens and hopelessness. All of the frivolity and prosperity of the '20s faded away, along with the expectations of a nation. Only Hollywood seemed to offer a respite.

Women who were little girls in the 1930s always mention the same two significant events that impacted their young lives: the Great Depression, and seeing Shirley Temple on the silver screen. Because of the first event, the majority of American mothers were recycling cotton flour sacks into necessarily simple dresses for their daughters. They did their best to produce attractive everyday frocks and aprons from the pastels and small flower prints that previously packaged baking ingredients. They had to wait until they had saved up enough of the same cotton fabric before they could start sewing. Accordingly, these resourceful moms reshaped fashion to suit history and economics.

Girls still wore dresses most of the time, even for play, but the fabrics were practical ones. To conserve the limited amount of fabric, sleeves became shorter and less puffy, skirts had more of an A-line shape, often with a single center pleat, and they were only as long as they absolutely had to be. As yardage requirements decreased dramatically, lace receded in its importance until it was barely noticeable on the edges of Peter Pan collars and sleeve cuffs. Like their mothers, children wore plain smock-like aprons of similar fabrics to protect their clothing when helping out with chores. Brown cotton stockings were worn for everyday.

For better everyday dresses, waffle pique was popular, and some rayon was available. But by far the most common fancy fabric was cotton organdy, which made dandy ruffles and perky sleeves when heavily starched. (Moms did a lot of ironing in those days.) Most women who could sew a garment together also were able to produce at least rudimentary embroidery, usually in the form of kittens and puppies done in outline stitch. Often these designs were traced from magazine artwork or came from iron-on transfers.

Joan's Mom Nina and Brother

Hairdos for little girls also became quite simple, usually with straight short hair parted on one side, and a big bow on the other side of the head for dress-up. A girl was considered to be very lucky if she had naturally curly hair.

Then along came little Shirley Temple, with her ringlets and dimpled smile that lit up a whole continent. Suddenly, all over America straight hair was tortured into curls, tuition for dance lessons was somehow saved up in sugar bowls, and little girls started to believe once more that they might be a princess in disguise, a "poor little rich girl," or a brave alpine orphan. Anything was possible, and it didn't matter if you were poor, as long as you had spunk.

Sue Hartwig

The War Years

As we grew up we often heard our parents talk about "the war years," as though there had only been one war, and it took place in the 1940s. We didn't realize then that war is present somewhere on the planet every second of every year, and has been since the dawn of history--perhaps a sad commentary on our species.

But while war brings out the worst in people, it also brings out the best. Magazines and books from the '40s were filled with the patriotic fervor and push for selflessness in the advertisements as well as articles. Celebrities hawked war bonds and blood drives, women were actually urged to get out and work to help the war effort (of course, only as long as the men were at war, but that's another issue), and national pride swelled as Americans saw themselves as "the good guys" in a global drama of unprecedented scope.

Movies were priced within the reach of all, and we became quite sophisticated about the glamorous East and West Coasts. No longer were people isolated by lack of information. Now everyone saw the world, at least the way Hollywood saw the world. Accordingly, knowledge of the current fashions became much more current. The big movie studios churned out dozens of box office hits

Jean's Sister Joyce, 1947

12

Teri Monchamp, 1948

Joan (right) and sister Jenny

Betsy McCall was our fashion leader. Each month we cut out the paper dolls from the magazine after our mothers had read it.

featuring actors who actually did participate as soldiers and fighter pilots in the war, unforgettable stories of romance and heroism. Frequently the love interest in the script was a nurse, so little girls aspired to the healing profession. This concept was reinforced by the omnipresent Red Cross posters featuring angels of mercy in nurses' caps. Shirley Temple wasn't so little anymore, but she was seen more than once on the silver screen in a nurse costume. Naturally, dolls followed suit.

The military look swept women's fashion, with padded shoulders and narrow waists simulating a masculine silhouette. Trousers were finally acceptable for women, but little girls still wore dresses most of the time. Middy blouses and sailor dresses became very popular, a salute to our Navy boys, and a very common color combination for children's clothing was red, white and blue. Another contribution from the war effort was the emergence of nylon fabric, which had been developed for parachutes. Nylon came to be viewed as a more modern substitute for cotton organdy.

Skirts remained nearly as short as they had been during the '30s, but they were much fuller. Little girls wore waist dresses most of the time now, with the short yokes reserved mainly for sailor dresses and toddler wear. Sleeves were often scaled down to a straight line, rather than being gathered. White cuffs and Peter Pan collars were everywhere, along with full, starched cotton or nylon pinafores. America definitely had her confidence back, and it showed in the bold and stylish clothing.

The Fabulous Fifties

This is probably our favorite era, because we were children then and everything seemed perfect. Not only had America vanquished the forces of evil as we saw them, she had become the symbol of economic prosperity. Moms went back to being "just" moms, dads went off to the office every day and came home every night to an orderly home and a plentiful dinner. At least that's how we saw ourselves, and how TV, the hypnotic cyclops that moved into our homes, saw us. We may not always have acted like those perfect families with their neat plot resolutions, but we sure did look like them.

Little girls were still wearing dresses most of the time, and they were still short as could be. Skirts were extra full, often boosted by crinoline and nylon net can-cans, impossibly scratchy contraptions that harkened back to the previous century when clothing was supposed to be uncomfortable. Often a skirt was coaxed out to a permanent twirl height by using gathered tiers, adding ever more fabric to the fullness. Waisted dresses were the norm, instead of yoke bodices, and prim Peter Pan collars went on everything, especially the ever-present white blouse. As for fabrics and colors, plaids and ginghams were the standard prints, with nylon organdy and velvet trim saved for holidays. Pink and gray was a very common color combination, not only for appliances, dinnerware and home decor, but also in the clothing of girls aged five to fifteen. Salmon pink and turquoise took over later in the decade as the "cool" colors. Just as penny loafers were part of a teenager's uniform in the '50s, Mary Janes, saddle shoes and white anklets were "must haves" to a pre-adolescent schoolgirl.

Although people in the '90s look back at the early second half of this century as a time when Americans were delusional and overly optimistic, for many of us they were indeed "Happy Days." Not that we want to go back to them, you understand, but we do look back on them fondly. We were able to spend time after school with our mothers, learning to cook and sew and keep a modern home... you know, all those things we rebelled against when we went off to college in the '60s.

The Sixties

Never had they seen so much skin!

Mini-skirts were downright...shall we say, "challenging" to wear. It is doubtful that males of that period had any idea how much planning and posturing were involved in wearing such revealing dresses in everyday life. Even little girls emulated their older sisters in this department. Interestingly, the amount of fabric needed for a mini was similar to that needed for a child's dress in the '30s. See those fashion cycles roll on and on!

Skirts were not only minuscule in length, they didn't have much fullness either. Older girls looked younger than they were, simply by virtue of the babyish length of their skirts. Dark tights compensated somewhat for the chill factor, but not much. Maybe that's why everybody had long hair--to keep warm! Later in the decade, the granny dress was all the rage. For some peculiar reason the granny dress was just an ankle-length version of the baby doll dress. Go figure.

For younger children and their dolls, these styles translated into fairly boring clothes--except for the colors. We called them "psychedelic," but now, 30 years later, we call them "neon." Either way, they certainly were noticeable. Paisley prints, gypsy shawls, fringes, beads and tie-dying. The more things change....

The Scandalous Seventies

Fashion-wise, the '70s were so embarrassing we decided to ignore them in terms of small children and dolls. This decade marked the emergence of the "Me Generation," or so it was called by the media. That's when federal funding of schools and general interest in the needs of children seemed to decline, and somehow that was reflected in fashion as well. There simply wasn't anything stylish about children's clothing. In fact, fashion stagnated during that decade, its only memorable contribution being bell bottomed pants, actually a holdover from the late '60s. For instance, Joan's "going away" outfit for her 1976 honeymoon was a lemon yellow polyester pantsuit.

As far as children's clothing was concerned, we seemed to be waiting for something really new and interesting to happen. We waited, and waited.... Meanwhile, little girls switched over to pants and tops--practical, but not very interesting on dolls.

Friend Laura Erickson and Grandpa, 1955

From a Simplicity pattern for "Penny Brite" Doll, 1965

Just think how many Polyesters died for this pantsuit! Meanwhile, Jean was struggling to walk in platform shoes.

14

Daughters Rebecca and
Margaret in the Victorian
reproduction dresses we made.

The Eighties

And the fashion world slumbered while the sports world gave us sweat suits. Lots of sweat suits, sweat suits with lace trim, sweat suits with fabric paint, sweat suits with zippers, sweat suits with glitter.

Maybe we got tired of waiting, so someone dragged out those dresses grandma used to wear as a child, and tried to duplicate them. Ta-dah! "Heirloom Sewing" was born. And we who like things dripping with lace and ribbons were ecstatic. Hemlines dropped, gathered skirts were once again full, little girls dressed up, and they even wore hats! Victorian floral prints were all the rage, along with pastel Swiss cottons trimmed with French laces. Several magazines that cater to smockers and embroiderers made their debut. The old needle arts, including lace-making, were revived. Turn-of-the-century ribbon work cascaded off infants' and dolls' dresses. Once we learned how to create these art forms ourselves, our appreciation for them grew.

This is where we came in. It's now the mid-nineties, and although little girls may be wearing blue jeans and oversize sweatshirts to school, they have developed their own appreciation for ribbons and lace and Victorian silhouettes. While they themselves may not want to be encumbered by these fancy get-ups on a daily basis, they do love to dress their dolls that way. And so do those of us who are already grown up, but are still playing with dolls.

Who's Who in the Color Tableaux
The Center Photos

Timeless Essentials: The Slumber Party

In this photo we see Hilary in her shortie nightie and scuffs about to comb out her hair. Her ruffled panties pattern is the same one used for all the dolls' unmentionables. Shay wears a flannel granny nightgown as she cuddles her teddy bear and prepares to read a bedtime story. May is taking out the curlers from her home permanent set. Sensibly, she wears only her petticoat for this messy procedure.

Jenny and Joan

The china Cinderella coach atop the wardrobe has become Fancywork and Fashion's logo, so we try to sneak it into each book somewhere. The patchwork quilt, Russian needlepunch rug, and doily coverlet were made by Jean's mom long ago. The Mother Goose book is a miniaturized color photocopy of a real book from Jean's childhood, enclosing a small piece of white cardboard. We don't know those strange women whose photographs are on the wall.

What Great Depression? Kitchen Warmth

This shot began with the ugliest stick-on floor tile we could find. Then we added simple items we scrounged from Jean's mom's old linens, a friend's playroom kitchen, and antique stores. The radio is a reproduction, and it really works. Even though the 1930s predates us, we got lots of input from Joan's mom and friends. The brown cotton stockings were apparently universally disliked.

Shirley samples a fresh cookie, wearing her famous smile and a yoke dress with detachable collar. Willow's flour sack dress is made more practical for the kitchen with the addition of a cotton apron. Jenny's yoke dress is similar to Willow's, but she has a kitty face apron, embellished with outline embroidery that any mother could learn to do. Emily is a more well-to-do neighbor who has stopped in to see what smells so good. Her ruffled dress is also modeled after those typically worn by Shirley Temple, but Emily's cloth thighs prevent her from wearing hers as short as Shirley's.

Colleen Klundt (Nina) and friends, 1937

The War Years: Everyone Must do Her Part!

In her full nurse's uniform, Georgia is about to administer a dose of medicine to her doll malingering beneath the flannel blankets. Christina, in her sailor dress, is just a flag-waver. Those dramatic Red Cross posters distress her too much! In her heart bib pinafore outfit, Heidi takes her job as nanny very seriously. The washing is done, but there's still ironing, and goodness--look at all those toys to pick up!

Yes, the Slinky was invented in the 1940s, believe it or not. Raggedy Ann and the red table and chair were loaned to us by Joan's mom Nina. The rest of the toys were begged and borrowed from various other sources. We especially liked the miniature poster stuck to the hospital bed. Incidentally, Heidi's shoes once belonged to Joan's daughter Rebecca.

The Military Influence

The Hub of the Home: The 1950s kitchen

There's that floor again. Auggggghhhhh! We were kids in the 1950s, so we went overboard with that decade. But that's our prerogative because it's our book and our memories, right?

So many of the magazines from the '50s featured pink appliance advertisements that when Joan found this fridge, stove and cupboard at our church rummage sale for $10, she scooped them up. We also couldn't resist recreating a Ford Edsel ad (it's fallen beneath the table in all the activity).

Hannah's yoke dress and teapot pinafore was a staple of that era. Angel's dotted nylon organdy dress has three lined tiers in its skirt to make it stick out to the maximum. And Tiffany's plaid waist dress seemed to be in every little girl's closet in the '50s.

Do You Have Time for a Cup of Tea? (Front Cover)

Bedtime Jenny is wide awake in her turquoise taffeta waist dress and nylon organdy pinafore. Patent leather Mary Janes and white anklets were mandatory with dress-up outfits in the fabulous fifties.

Joan was domestic even in the 1950s.

Jean and Toni Doll (the one in curlers), 1955

Joan and friends, first day of school

Joan's Prom dress, 1967

Weren't All the Best Pop Christmas Tunes Recorded in the Fifties? (Back Cover)

Anne feels especially festive in her pink nylon organdy Special Dress. Maybe it's the black velveteen bodice that makes it so extra dressy. Maybe it's that artificial flower at her waist. (Joan's mother always removed the fake rose-buds that frequently embellished her daughter's store-bought dresses as soon as they got home. In her opinion, they made the dress look cheap.) Or was it the pink pearl buttons? Or could it be that silver aluminum tree behind her?

The Neighborhood School in the '50s

Oh, those endless penmanship exercises. Nowadays the kids get away with keyboarding repetitions. Remember those warm wooden floors and the smell of the waxes and chalk dust and purple mimeograph ink? Back then the school music books were full of rousing patriotic songs and traditional American folk tunes. And every classroom had a picture of George Washington and the current President. (George is on the wall you can't see.)

Willow's plaid shirtwaist is so spiffy with lots of red Rick Rack and special apple shaped buttons. Her carefully polished saddle shoes complete her well-groomed look. Emily looks even more prim in her crisp white blouse and knife pleated plaid skirt and suspenders. A little ribbon bow at the neck is always nice. Shay's mother learned how to smock recently, so she whipped up this blue gingham frock for school.

The '60s Basement Recreation Room

We hate to say it, but the nineties have definitely borrowed a few fashion tips from the sixties. Like those very short dresses. Maybe it has something to do with all those "oldies" radio stations on the air today. We just can't seem to get away from the good old days. Actually, the best part of that time period was that basement recreation rooms became popular and kids could get away from their parents (and vice versa). Again, we suspect it had something to do with the music. All you had to do was put up some cheap paneling or some of that lovely (choke) daisy print wallpaper, move the old sofa and some beanbag chairs down there and you were all set. A TV and lava lamp were icing on the cake. Incidentally, those are 1960 Presidential debate reruns they're watching. This was the decade when our youth became intensely interested in politics, you know.

May's Carnaby Street "Op Art" dress is as short as can be. Except for the fact that it's a mini, it bears a striking resemblance to Joan's senior prom dress. Hilary's baby doll dress is definitely back in style in the nineties. She even crocheted her own vest and strung her own beads. With flowers in her hair and rose colored glasses, even this room looks good to her. Pui Ling is a younger sister who still likes the white blouse and jumper look, but she has chosen denim for the jumper. And there are those darn daisies again on her skirt. Not to mention trolls--boy they seem familiar, don't they?

Fashion Revolution in the Eighties

Although the sixties and seventies launched us permanently into the blue jeans mode, little girls do still dress up occasionally. But the skirts have definitely gotten longer. Elegant lace came back in the 1980s and smocking enjoyed a definite rebirth. Bold new fabric prints came out that made people who had never sewn before flock to fabric stores. There they found lots of new craft materials such as fabric paints, wire-edged ribbons and tons of how-to books for mothers with not a lot of leisure time. A new, bolder, neo-Victorian look allowed for more creative license in children's clothing. And children started to really have a say in their own garment choices--sometimes their ensembles are more than creative!

Georgia contemplates her croquet strategy in her sunflower dress with detached blossom collar and floppy hat to protect her from the sun. Heidi's garden pinafore is very practical on a hot day, but she's taking an ice cream break right now, thank you. Elise's strawberry print yoke dress has a strawberry-shaped pocket. (Black background prints became very popular in the late eighties and early nineties.)

Jean's Daughter Margaret

The 1990s: Victorian Fashions With Real Flair

There's definitely been a renaissance of turn-of-the-century fashions, but we've made them our own with bolder color choices and an array of companion print fabrics and laces that were previously unavailable. Grandmother would be proud!

Shy Violet's party dress is made possible by a lovely border print fabric and Cluny lace. A craft store hat with ribbon around the brim shaded her fair complexion on her way to the tea party. Christina's candy striped taffeta dress and scalloped pinafore show off her mother's handiwork--embroidered rosebuds and some French machine sewing techniques. Elise is proud of her mother's smocking too. Yes, you can smock on a busy floral background and get a very pretty result. Her lace-trimmed floppy hat has a bow that matches her dress. And Angel's Sunday best is a work of heirloom art. Turn to the Basic Instructions for French Machine Sewing Techniques to learn these simple methods of creating frothy lace confections.

Joan's Daughter Rebecca and friend,
and Son Kevin

Jean and friend with
sister Joyce

Chapter 3

So You Know What Kind of Costume to Make—What Now?

The Concept Behind Modern Doll Costuming

Whether you are making outfits for your granddaughter's vinyl doll that gets dragged everywhere, or you are finally dealing with the fact that you've painted eight porcelain dolls in a studio class and they're all still naked, modern dolls are some of the easiest to sew for. First of all, you don't have to worry about using authentic closures for a particular time period, whether or not you can use synthetic fabric, or if the style you pick is really historically accurate--unless you are entering a competition. In other words, you don't have to do any research to come up with a very rewarding project that will be met with approval by all parties concerned when you get it done. You can do what you want.

Playable Dolls (The Ones Children Have)

If the doll is meant to be played with, the costume should be sturdy and washable. Dresses that have no center back seam at all but have Velcro strips are easier for small children to use. Some people object to the use of Velcro, however, because it catches on lace and doll wigs. Snaps are the logical alternative. For young ones, the watchword is simplify, simplify, simplify. Make it easy on yourself, because in a child's eyes, a finished garment with shortcuts is better than a perfectly unfinished one.

Playable Dolls (The Ones You Keep For Yourself)

Many, many people tell us they are collecting all the vinyl dolls they can for themselves, not for any child. They admit to playing with them too. These people are just like the ones who paint and/or collect modern porcelain dolls. They tend to take great pride in the actual designing and planning of doll costumes, may invest more money in the supplies, and expend much more effort in the embellishment, props and accessories. Some of you are real maniacs--you know who you are.

Often people start out in the first category, dutifully making clothes for their daughter's dolls. And then when they're not paying close attention to reality, they lose all control and start keeping dolls and their costumes for themselves. It's not as expensive as going to a casino, but you can see the same glassy look in their eyes when you try to talk to them about practical things, like maybe starting dinner or getting the laundry done. They have become doll addicts.

Well, so what. It's a pretty harmless addiction, and it's cheaper than therapy. Go for it.

Happy adult sewing
for her doll

Chapter 4

You Must Read This Before You Sew!

Basic Construction Techniques

If you have used any of our other pattern books, you'll recognize much of the following information. Nevertheless, you can save yourself some aggravation if you scan it before you begin one of our costumes. We try to pack as many patterns into a book for a reasonable price as we possibly can, so our style is to first give you a generalized introduction to our dress construction techniques used in nearly all the doll dresses we design. Then specific garment instructions will follow in the order the outfits appear in the color photographs. After all, as we said before, a dress is a dress is a dress, so we think it's wasteful of time and paper to reprint the same basic construction steps for every single garment.

So here's all you really need to know about putting together these outfits.

1.   **How to use the patterns.** The pattern pieces included in this book are designed to be traced onto plain white typing paper or tracing paper. Cut out the traced pieces and store them in an envelope. Be sure to copy all pertinent instructions such as fold lines and *'s.

2.   **Seams.** To make a seam, pin the fabric pieces right sides together, stitch and press seam allowance to one side. All pattern pieces include 1/4" seam allowances. It's up to you whether you choose to finish off the seam allowances, but we recommend zig-zagging or serging anything that seems likely to ravel.

French seams are not necessary unless you are working with transparent fabrics like organdy. To make a French seam, pin the fabric pieces wrong sides together, stitch 1/8" away from the raw edges, turn so that the fabric pieces are right sides together, press and stitch, enclosing the raw edges of the first stitching within the seam. Press to one side.

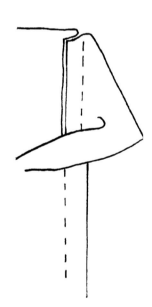

French seam

Special Doll Costuming Hint: When making seams where you will want to trim away the seam allowance very close to the stitching line, use shorter stitches, such as 1.5 mm. This will allow closer trimming with less risk of the remaining fabric fraying into nothingness. This works especially well when doing small pieces like collars. We thank our seamstress Karen Cermak for this forehead-slapper. (You know, one of those "Why didn't I think of that myself?" ideas.)

3.   **Bodice/yoke construction.** The bodice is the part of the dress or blouse that covers the torso from neck to waist. It is what you have in a "waisted dress." The yoke is just a shorter version of a bodice, covering the torso from neck to somewhere just below the underarm. It is what you have in a "yoke dress."

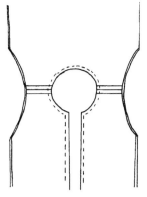

Bodice/Yoke
Construction

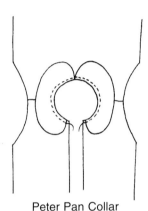

Peter Pan Collar

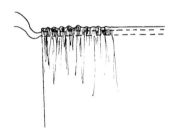

Gathering

Our quick and easy lined bodice/yoke construction method eliminates the need to work with tiny facings and complicated plackets. Here are the steps you need to follow in nearly every dress or blouse in this book:

Cut out two fronts and four backs if it opens in the back, or four fronts and two backs if it opens in the front. Stitch back to front at shoulders. Repeat for lining.

Then place the bodice/yoke and its lining right sides together and stitch around the neck edges and down the center backs (or fronts, if it opens in the front). Clip curves, turn right side out and press. If you feel like being really precise, or are dealing with particularly slippery fabric, baste the bodice/yoke and lining together around all the remaining edges so it's easier to treat it as one unit. Do not sew the side seams until the sleeves are attached.

4.   **Peter Pan Collars.** Cut out four from pattern piece, if the blouse/dress opens in the back. Otherwise, for a front-opening garment, cut out two from the one-piece Peter Pan pattern. Both of these come in two sizes, medium and small, for some variation. Be sure you are cutting out the one called for.

Right sides together, sew collar to lining around outside edge of collar pieces. Here's one of those places where it's a great idea to use a smaller stitch so you can trim away seam allowance closer than you normally dare. Turn right side out and press. Apply to garment as instructed in individual pattern instructions.

5.   **Gathering**. Most of these garments require some gathering, usually sleeves and skirts. Taking a little extra time with it pays off in the final look of a garment. For those who haven't sewn much before, in order to gather you feed the fabric through the machine, right side up, stitch length set extra long. You will pull the bobbin thread to cause the ruffled effect.

Even though you are dealing with 1/4" seams, make two rows of gathering anyway. The gathering will turn out much more even than if you use one row, and also you have a backup in case one of the threads breaks. Make the first gathering line right along the 1/4" seam line, putting the second one 1/8" closer to the edge of the fabric. Make the seam right on top of the first gathering line.

6.   **Sleeve Construction--Three Styles.** Of course, all styles of sleeve can be made in any length according to your choice, but the sleeves shown in all of our photographs are either short (suitable only for all porcelain or compo bodies) or medium. In the instructions called "What to do for other dolls," we may tell you to use the Short or Medium Sleeve pattern. You must make this choice based on how much the cloth part of your doll's arm may extend down. Incidentally, we have used the long sleeve pattern only for the granny nightgown, but of course you may use it on any dress you please.

Elastic Sleeve Bottom with Ruffle

a.   Zig-zag or serge the bottom edge of the sleeve hem, then turn it up and stitch by machine. OR use your rolled hem attachment. Or, for a variation, turn the fabric up 1/8" and attach narrow lace by pinning the heading of the lace to the folded-under fabric, then top stitching.

b.   Cut two pieces of 1/8" wide elastic as specified in the individual patterns. Using a pencil, draw a line on the wrong side of the sleeve 1/2" to 3/4" above and parallel to the hemmed sleeve bottom. Using two or three straight stitches, anchor one end of the elastic to the fabric on the line. Switch to a wide enough zig-zag stitch to swing back and forth over the elastic, creating a mini-casing. Stretch the elastic as you proceed to the end of the line; straight stitch the elastic to the fabric to anchor it at the end.

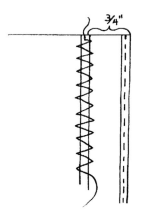

Elastic Sleeve Bottom
With Ruffle

Puffed Sleeve With Narrow Binding

a.   Gather the bottom edge of the sleeve. Cut out two strips of fabric on the bias, using the width and length recommended in the individual patterns for specific doll bodies.

b.   Pull the gathering threads of the sleeve to fit the bias binding. Right side of bias to wrong side of sleeve, sew the binding to the bottom edge of the sleeve. If the fabric has a lot of body, trim away some of the seam allowance.

c.   Press the remaining long edge of the bias 1/4" toward the wrong side of the fabric and fold the entire binding around to the right side of the sleeve. Top stitch along the folded edge of the binding.

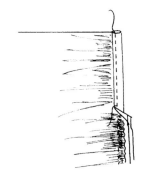

Puffed Sleeve With Narrow Binding

Gathered Sleeve With Cuff

Follow instructions for puffed sleeve with narrow binding, except cut the binding on grain (not on the bias) and wider, as indicated in the specific pattern instructions.

7.   Sewing Sleeve to Bodice/Yoke. Gather the sleeve caps between *'s marked on the pattern piece. Right sides together, stitch sleeve to armhole of garment.

Only then will you sew the underarm seam. Never sew a doll garment's sleeve seam and then try to set it in. We learned this the hard way.

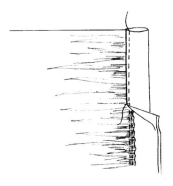

Gathered Sleeve With Cuff

8.   **Center back openings.** For playable dolls owned by very young children, you might consider an option we recommended in our first two books: leave the entire center back open. Simply hem the center back edges as described in #9 below all the way down to the bottom of the garment. No matter how tiny the fingers, they will be able to dress the doll all by themselves, saving frustration for the child and time for you.

However, you will want to make a center back seam for most "display" dolls. Because all the dolls and dress styles are so different, it's too hard to give specific lengths of the seam, but you should leave the garment open above the hip line so you can get the dress over the doll's head or up over her hips. In this size range three to four inches down from the top edge of the skirt is usually sufficient. When in doubt, leave it open a bit more than you think is necessary.

Underarm Seam

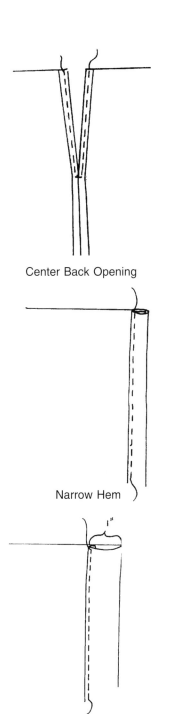

Center Back Opening

Narrow Hem

Hemming the Bottom of a Dress

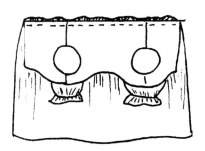

Attaching Skirt to Bodice

After you have sewn the center back seam as far up as you think you should (backstitching at the end of the seam, of course), press the remaining seam allowance toward the wrong side of the garment 1/4". You can serge this seam allowance and just leave it as is. Or, you can top stitch as though you were installing a zipper, starting at the top of the skirt, going along the center back opening, making a square "U" shape at the bottom, and stitching back up the other side. The self-lined bodice will be ready to attach directly to this hemmed "placket."

9.   **Hems.** All skirt lengths have been calculated based on styles of the decade, decency, and perhaps the most annoying factor, how far down cloth legs extend before they meet porcelain. Sometimes you cannot have a skirt as short as it should be for a particular time period because the cloth body would show.

Remember that you have 1-1/4" hem allowance on all dresses, except those with lace on the bottom. Perhaps you don't like how short we've made the dresses, perhaps your doll has longer legs and needs a longer skirt. Do a little measuring before you cut the skirt out to avert disaster. Perhaps you are using the pattern for one era, but want the skirt length of a different time period. Remember that old carpenter's adage, "Measure twice, cut once."

Hems can be done by machine in most cases.

When we say "hem the center back edges" of a garment, we mean you should turn the raw edge 1/4" towards the wrong side of the fabric, turn it under another 1/4" and stitch.

When we say "narrow hem" something, like the bottom of a ruffled sleeve, or the bottom of a skirt ruffle, turn the fabric towards the wrong side 1/8" and press. Turn it under another 1/8" and stitch. Another method is to use your narrow hemmer attachment on your sewing machine. This handy little item is especially useful with filmy fabrics. Consult your machine's instruction book and try this wherever you want a rolled-hem effect.

When we say "hem the bottom of the dress," we mean you should turn the fabric toward the wrong side 1/4" and press. Turn it up 1" more and stitch. Except where the bottom of a dress consists of a ruffle, all the skirt lengths in these patterns include this 1-1/4" hem.

10.   **Attaching skirts to bodices.** This should be the last procedure done on your doll dress, other than embellishments and fasteners. Run gathering stitches around the top of the skirt. Mark the center front of the bodice and the skirt so you can match those points and distribute the gathering evenly between the two halves of the dress.

Pull the gathering thread to fit the skirt to the bodice. Right sides together, stitch with the skirt on top so you can watch and manipulate the gathers. Stitch right on top of the 1/4" gathering line.

Trim away excess seam allowance and zig-zag or serge.

11. **French Machine Sewing Techniques**

a. **Flat Lace Insertion to Flat Insertion or Gathered Lace.** Right sides up, piece of lace parallel to each other, zig-zag with a fine stitch so that the needle swings back and forth over the edge of both parts. This same method is used to attach gathered lace edging to flat lace insertion. The only difference is that you pull the gathering thread of the lace edging to gather it first.

b. **Flat Lace Edging to Flat Fabric.** Right sides together, place the lace 1/8" from the raw edge of the fabric. Zig-zag with a fine stitch. The excess fabric will roll up into the seam allowance. Open out and press.

c. **Entredeux to Flat Fabric.** Determine which side of the entredeux is the right side. It should be more smooth than the wrong side. Trim away all but 1/8" of the fabric from one side of the entredeux. Right sides together with trimmed edge of entredeux flush with raw fabric edge, straight stitch right next to the "ladder" along the outside edge of the entredeux. Using a tight zig-zag, overcast this tiny seam allowance. Open and press seam toward fabric.

d. **Entredeux to Gathered Fabric.** This technique is frequently used on gathered sleeves. The technique is the same as c. above, but the fabric is gathered first.

e. **Gathered Lace Edging to Entredeux.** Trim away all fabric from one side of the entredeux. Pull the gathering thread of the lace to fit the entredeux. Right sides up, carefully zig-zag into each hole of the entredeux, swinging the needle back over the heading of the lace.

a. Flat Lace Insertion to
Flat Insertion or Gathered Lace

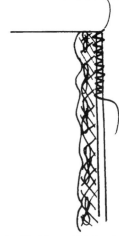

b. Flat Lace Edging to Flat Fabric

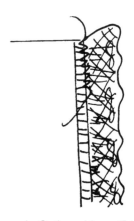

d. Gathered Lace Edging
to Entredeux

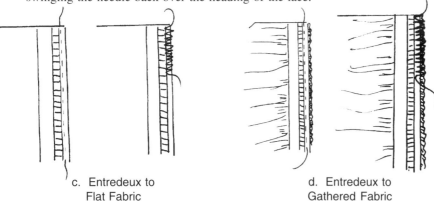

c. Entredeux to
Flat Fabric

d. Entredeux to
Gathered Fabric

f. Smocking Stitches

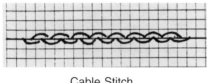

Cable Stitch

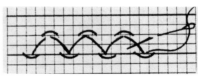

Trellis Stitch

24

Yoke Bodice

Waist Bodice

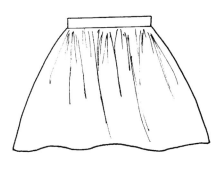

Sleeve

Chapter 5

The Patterns

These patterns have a system you need to understand before you begin. Remember what we said earlier? That a dress is a dress is a dress. There is a bodice (usually with sleeves) and a skirt. We have a simplified system of putting those parts together so that you can enjoy the planning and embellishment of your creations, rather than learning a whole new set of construction details for each garment. Therefore, in each outfit pattern you are referred back to our Basic Instructions, where we tell you how to sew the bodice together, how to make the sleeves, and how to sew on the skirt (which, in this book, always starts out as a rectangle shape). Why should that be repeated for each dress if it is basically the same? After you've sewn a couple dresses from this book you won't even have to refer back to the Basic Instructions, because the concept is so simple.

So you know how each dress is put together, but how do you make it in the size you need?

For the sake of clarity, we have first given instructions for the dresses pictured as though you were sewing for the same size and type of dolls shown wearing them in our photos. When you sew the same dress for a different size doll, you will cut out pattern pieces appropriate for the new doll and follow specific instructions for that doll as indicated. The other dolls are listed in order of size, from smallest to largest. Those instructions specific to the new size doll usually have to do with skirt length and sleeve cuff size. So be sure that you find the correct pattern pieces for your doll and make the necessary modifications within the instructions.

One comment about sleeve and skirt lengths. As a general rule, the dresses of the 1930s, '40s and '50s were as short as could be. The sleeves also tended to be very short (a lot of cardigan sweaters were sold in those days). But you know as well as we do that many of these dolls would look ridiculous in really short sleeves and skirts because the joint between cloth body and porcelain hand or leg would detract from the appearance of the doll. Therefore, we have given you the shortest size sleeve pattern and skirt length workable for each doll body. If you put these doll heads on all porcelain bodies, go for the shortest you can. But if you are using the bodies recommended by the sculptor, you can count on our recommended sleeve lengths to at least cover those unsightly joints.

About waistband lengths: We costume our dolls while they are in under-the-arm stands. Therefore, waistband lengths include enough fabric to include the stand. If you are using another style stand or for some reason do not want to include it in the garment, measure the doll's waist and add 3/4" to determine waistband length.

Finally, remember that 1/4" seam allowances are included in all pattern pieces.

Skirt

Hilary's Shortie Nightie, Panties and Scuffs

(Hilary's body is the T.J. 501)

Supplies:

1/2 yd. dotted Swiss fabric
1 yd. elastic, 1/8" wide
1 yd galloon for straps, or ribbon, any width
2 yd. flat eyelet lace, 1/2" wide
2 small snaps
Scrap of felt for scuffs
Fabric stiffener
1/3 yd. elastic, 1/4" wide
Two 1" pom-poms

PANTIES: First things first!

Cut out two from Small Panties pattern, on fold. Press the lower straight edges 1/4" toward the wrong side. Place heading of flat lace underneath the fold of the fabric and stitch. Cut two pieces of 1/8" elastic each 4" long. Zig-zag to wrong side of each leg, 1/2" above the junction of lace and fabric, using Basic Instructions for Elastic Sleeve Bottom with Ruffle.

Right sides together, sew center front and center back seams. Sew inner leg seam.

Press top edge of panties 1/4" toward inside of garment. Press under another 1/4" and stitch along very edge of folded fabric to form casing, leaving opening at center back to insert elastic. Thread enough 1/8" elastic through the casing to fit snugly around the waist and secure.

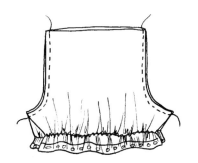

Center Front and
Center Back Seams

WHAT TO DO FOR OTHER DOLLS

The following dolls use the same pattern piece (labeled Small Panties) and leg elastic measurements as Hilary: *Christina, Violet, Shirley, May, Angel.*

The following dolls use the Medium Panties pattern piece and 5" elastic in each leg: *Götz/Pleasant Co., Elise, Georgia, Tiffany, Emily, Jenny.*

The following dolls use the Large Panties pattern piece and 6" elastic in each leg: *Shay, Willow, Heidi.*

SHORTIE NIGHTIE

Cut out a rectangle for the skirt 5-1/4" X 36". Narrow hem the two center back edges. Finish the bottom edge of the nightie by pressing one long edge under 1/4". Placing the heading of the lace underneath the fold, right sides up, sew lace to bottom of nightie.

Gather the top edge of the nightie.

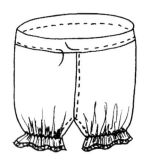

Elastic Casing

Cut a narrow band of the fabric 2-1/2" X 11-1/4". Right sides together, fold the band in half lengthwise. Stitch across the short ends. Turn band right side out and press. Right sides together, sew the band to the gathered skirt.

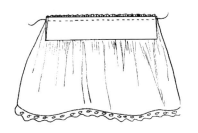

Sew Band to
Gathered Skirt

To trim the band, sew a piece of galloon to it, tucking in the ends 1/4". Depending upon the embroidery of the galloon itself, decide where to run the stitching lines.

For straps, cut two pieces of galloon 5" long. Mark the center of the nightie's top band, measure 1/2" from the center on both sides. These new markings are where one side of the strap will be attached. Stitch strap in place along previous stitching. Try the nightie on to determine length of the straps needed, pin in place, then stitch as you did in the front, 1/2" from the center backs.

Lapping right over left, sew two snaps to the center back.

SCUFFS

Make a pattern of your doll's feet by tracing around them, right and left. Believe it or not, some dolls actually have differently shaped feet so you can't always count on being able to just flip them over to get the opposite foot.

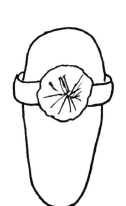

Scuff

From felt, cut out two soles for each foot. Soak the felt in fabric stiffener and allow it to dry overnight. When the soles are dry, mark one set of them 1/2" from the front of the sole on both sides; these are the innersoles. This is where the elastic will go over the top of the foot. Measure over the top of the doll's foot from mark to mark and add 1". Cut two pieces of 1/4" elastic this measurement. Using fabric glue, attach the ends of the elastic to the bottom side of the innersoles, each end extending about 1/2" in from the edges. Glue a matching sole to the bottom of each scuff. Glue a pom-pom to the center of each elastic strap.

WHAT TO DO FOR OTHER DOLLS

Shirley: Skirt is 5" X 32"; band is 10-1/4" long; straps are 5" each.
Violet: Skirt is 4-1/4" X 36; band is 11-1/4" long; straps are 5-1/2" each.
Götz/Pleasant Co.: Skirt is 5-1/4" X 38"; band is 12-1/4" long; straps are 6" each.
Christina/T.J. 512: Follow Hilary's instructions exactly.
Angel/May: Skirt is 5-1/4" X 36"; band is 11-3/4" long; straps are 5-1/2" each.
Jenny/Emily: Skirt is 6-1/4" X 40"; band is 13-1/4" long; straps are 6" each.
Elise/Georgia: Skirt is 6" X 40"; band is 12-3/4" long; straps are 6" each.
Shay: Skirt is 5-1/2" X 36"; band is 11" long; straps are 5-1/2" each.
Tiffany: Skirt is 7" X 36"; band is 11-3/4" long; straps are 6-1/2" each.
Willow: Skirt is 7" X 45"; band is 14-3/4" long; straps are 5-1/2" each.
Heidi: Skirt is 7" X 45"; band is 14-3/4" long; straps are 7" each.

Shay's Granny Nightgown

(Shay's body is from the pattern provided by the mold company.)

Supplies:

1 yd. flannel fabric
16" flat eyelet lace, 1/2"-5/8" wide
1-1/4 yd. flat eyelet lace, 1" wide
1/4 yd. elastic, 1/8" wide
3 decorative heart buttons
3 snaps

BODICE

Cut out two fronts and four backs using Yoke Dress bodice pieces. Assemble bodice and bodice lining according to Basic Instructions, but do not sew lining to bodice yet.

Gather the 16" of narrower eyelet lace and pin it to the yoke neckline, right sides together and short ends folded under 1/4". Baste in place.

Right sides together, sew lining to bodice, sandwiching lace between them, stitching up the center backs and around the neckline, just as you would normally sew the bodice together.

Cut out two sleeves using Long Sleeve pattern piece with Elastic Cutting Line. Assemble sleeves according to Basic Instructions for Elastic Sleeve Bottom with Ruffle, using 3-1/2" elastic for each sleeve. Attach sleeves to bodice and then sew underarm sleeves according to Basic Instructions.

Gather 40" of the wide eyelet and stitch it to the lower edge of the bodice, right sides together and short ends of the lace folded under 1/4". Baste.

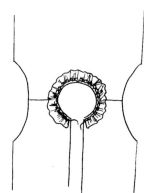

Attaching Gathered
Lace to Bodice

SKIRT

Cut out a rectangle 10-1/4" X 35". Cut out a ruffle 3" X 70" (this needs to be pieced, of course). Narrow hem one long edge of the ruffle. Gather the remaining long edge of the ruffle and sew it, right sides together, to one long edge of the skirt. Sew the center back opening as instructed in Basic Instructions #9. Gather and sew the skirt to the bodice as directed in Basic Instructions #10, sandwiching the eyelet between the two.

Sew snaps to center back, lapping right over left. Sew three decorative heart buttons to center front of nightgown.

WHAT TO DO FOR OTHER DOLLS

Shirley: Skirt: 8" X 28"; ruffle: 2" X 56"; 12" narrow eyelet, 25" wide eyelet; 2-3/4" elastic per sleeve; only 2 decorative buttons.
Violet: Skirt: 7-1/2" X 28"; ruffle: 2" X 56"; 16" narrow eyelet, 30" wide eyelet; 3" elastic per sleeve; only 2 decorative buttons.
Götz/Pleasant Co.: Skirt: 8" X 36"; 3-3/4" elastic per sleeve; rest is same as

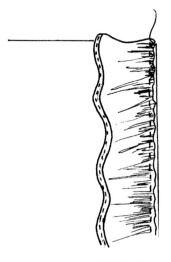

Skirt Ruffle

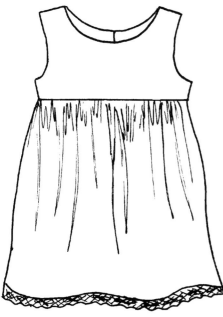

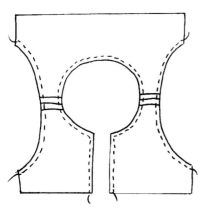

Stitch Bodice and Lining
Together Around
Armholes

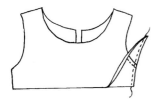

Stitching Side Seams

Shay.

Hilary/T.J. 501: Skirt: 9" X 36"; 2-3/4" elastic per sleeve; rest is same as Shay.

Christina/T.J. 512: Skirt 10-1/2" X 36"; 2-3/4" elastic per sleeve; rest is the same as Shay.

Angel/May: Skirt: 9" X 36"; 2-3/4" elastic per sleeve; rest is the same as Shay.

Elise: Skirt: 10" X 36"; 2-3/4" elastic per sleeve; rest is the same as Shay.

Georgia: Skirt: 11" X 36"; 2-3/4" elastic per sleeve; rest is the same as Shay.

Emily/Jenny: Skirt: 9" X 36"; 3" elastic per sleeve; rest is the same as Shay.

Tiffany: Exactly the same as Shay.

Willow: Skirt: 12-1/2" X 40"; ruffle: 3" X 80"; 16" narrow eyelet, 45" wide eyelet; 2-3/4" elastic per sleeve.

Heidi: Skirt: 11" X 40"; ruffle: 3" X 80"; 16" narrow eyelet, 45" wide eyelet; 3-3/4" elastic per sleeve.

May's Petticoat

(May's body is Seeley's composition MB140S 14")

<u>Supplies:</u>

1/2 yd. batiste
1 yd. flat lace, 1/2" wide
1 snap

Note that the skirt length given for this petticoat is suitable for the more modern dresses, which tend to be longer. If you are putting the petticoat underneath a dress from the '30s, '40s or '50s, you may well have to shorten it, as we did for the one shown in the photo. The petticoat should generally run 1" shorter than the hemmed dress. Make sure you determine this length before you proceed to sew, because the petticoat has a lace bottom, not a hem that can easily be altered. In the section marked "What to do for other dolls," we have given you slip lengths for each doll to go with the modern dress lengths (longer).

BODICE

Cut out two fronts and four backs, using Jumper Yoke pattern pieces. Right sides together, sew each front to two backs at the shoulder seams, so that you have a bodice and a bodice lining.

Right sides together, sew the bodice to its lining by stitching along the center back edges and around the neckline. Then stitch bodice and lining together around armholes. Clip curves and trim seam allowances. Turn right side out by pulling the backs through the shoulder seams. Press.

Stitch the side seams together by opening up the bodice and lining at the armholes. Press and set aside.

SKIRT

Cut out a rectangle 8" X 30". Apply the flat lace to one long edge of the skirt (the bottom edge) by either using French machine lace-to-fabric technique, or press under the fabric 1/4", place the heading of the lace underneath and stitch.

Sew center back seam according to Basic Instructions #8.

Right sides together, sew bodice to skirt according to Basic Instructions #10. Sew snap to back neck.

WHAT TO DO FOR OTHER DOLLS

Shirley: Skirt is 6" X 22"; 22" flat lace.
Violet: Skirt is 5" X 24"; 24" flat lace.
Götz/Pleasant Co.: Skirt is 7" X 30"; 30" flat lace.
Hilary/T.J. 501/Christina/T.J. 512: Skirt is 7" X 30"; 30" flat lace.
Jenny/Emily: Skirt is 8-1/4" X 30"; 30" flat lace.
Angel: Follow May's instructions exactly.
Elise/Georgia: Skirt is 8-1/2" X 30"; 30" flat lace.
Shay: Skirt is 8-1/2" X 30"; 30" flat lace.
Tiffany: Skirt is 8-1/4" X 30"; 30" flat lace.
Willow: Skirt is 10-1/4" X 35"; 35" flat lace.
Heidi: Skirt is 9" X 35"; 35" flat lace.

Shirley's Yoke Dress With Center Pleat and Detached Collar

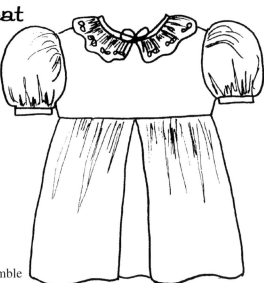

(Shirley's body is Scioto Character Body #623, completed doll is 16")

Supplies:

2/3 yd. fabric
1/2 yd. flat eyelet lace 1-1/2" wide
1/3 yd. ribbon 1/4" wide
1/4 yd. single fold bias tape for collar
3 small snaps

BODICE

Cut out two fronts and four backs using Yoke Dress bodice pieces. Assemble bodice according to Basic Instructions.

Cut out two sleeves using Short Sleeve pattern piece with Cuff Cutting Line and two bias strips 1" X 4" for sleeve binding.

Assemble sleeves according to Basic Instructions for Puffed Sleeve with Narrow Binding. Attach sleeves to bodice and then sew underarm sleeves according to Basic Instructions.

SKIRT

WARNING: This skirt is short short! The dimensions given for skirts are the shortest possible for the dolls listed. If in doubt, measure first. See the section

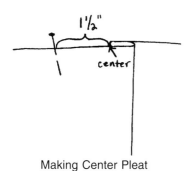

Making Center Pleat

Enclosing Gathered
Eyelet Lace in Bias
Tape

Finished Collar With Bow

under Hems in the Basic Instructions regarding skirt lengths appropriate for different types of dolls.

Cut a rectangle 6" X 24". Sew center back seam and hem skirt bottom as directed in Basic Instructions.

Make one box pleat in center front of skirt by doing the following: Mark the center front of the skirt on the unhemmed edge. Measure 1-1/2" on both sides of the center and mark those places with pins. With the right side of the skirt facing you, bring the pins to the center mark and baste the pleat in place.

Gather and attach the skirt according to Basic Instructions, #10. Lapping right back over left back, sew two snaps to dress bodice.

DETACHED COLLAR

Gather the top edge of the eyelet lace. Turn the short ends of the lace 1/4" toward the wrong side.

Cut the single fold bias tape so it is 7" long. Pull the gathering thread on the wrong side of the eyelet lace so that it fits the bias tape with the tape extending 1/4" on each end, wrong side of lace to right side of tape. Stitch in the fold of the tape.

Fold the short ends of the bias tape in and fold the long edge of the bias tape over to the right side of the eyelet lace, enclosing the raw edge of the lace. Top stitch along the folded edge of the bias tape.

Sew one snap to bias binding of collar, lapping right over left. Tie ribbon into neat bow and tack in place over the snap.

WHAT TO DO FOR OTHER DOLLS

All dolls use Short or Medium Sleeve pattern with Cuff Cutting Line.

Violet: Sleeve bias bindings are 1" X 4-1/4". The skirt is 5-3/4" X 28". The Detachable Collar's bias tape is 8" long.
Götz/Pleasant Co.: Sleeve bias bindings are 1" X 5". The skirt is 7-1/4" X 30". The Detachable Collar's bias tape is 8-1/2" long.
Hilary/T.J. 501: Sleeve bias bindings are 1" X 4". The skirt is 7" X 30". The Detachable Collar's bias tape is 7" long.
Jenny/Emily: Sleeve bias bindings are 1" X 4-1/4". The skirt is 8-3/4" X 30". The Detachable Collar's bias tape is 7" long.
Angel/May/Seeley ALB9873/MB140S 14": Sleeve bias bindings are 1" X 4-1/4". The skirt is 7-3/4" X 30". The Detachable Collar's bias tape is 7" long.
Christina/T.J. 512: Sleeve bias bindings are 1" X 4". The skirt is 7-3/4" X 30". The Detachable Collar's bias tape is 7" long.
Elise/Georgia: Sleeve bias bindings are 1" X 4-1/2". The skirt is 8-3/4" X 30". The Detachable Collar's bias tape is 7" long.
Shay: Sleeve bias bindings are 1" X 5-1/4". The skirt is 8-3/4" X 36". The Detachable Collar's bias tape is 7" long.
Tiffany: Sleeve bias bindings are 1" X 5". The skirt is 9" X 36". The Detachable Collar's bias tape is 7-1/2" long.

Willow: Sleeve bias bindings are 1" X 4-1/2". The skirt is 11-1/2" X 36" and you make the center pleat by measuring 2" in each direction from the center. The Detachable Collar's bias tape is 7" long.

Heidi: Sleeve bias bindings are 1" X 5-3/4". The skirt is 9" X 40" and you make the center pleat by measuring 2" in each direction from the center. The Detachable Collar's bias tape is 7" long.

Willow's Flour Sack Dress and Apron With Pockets

(Willow's body is from the pattern provided by the mold company.)

Supplies:

2/3 yd. dress fabric
Scrap of white broadcloth for collar
1/4 yd. gingham (1/16" size check) for apron
1 package white single fold bias tape
Red, green and brown embroidery floss
2 small snaps

BODICE

Cut out two fronts and four backs using Yoke Dress bodice pieces. Assemble bodice and bodice lining according to Basic Instructions, but do not sew lining to bodice yet.

Cut out four Medium Peter Pan Collar pieces from the white broadcloth as indicated on the pattern and assemble according to Basic Instructions for Peter Pan Collars.

Place collar on the right side of the bodice as shown and baste to bodice neckline.

Right sides together, sew lining to bodice, sandwiching collar between them, stitching up the center backs and around the neckline, just as you would normally sew the bodice together even if there were no collar there.

Cut out two sleeves using Medium Sleeve pattern piece with Cuff Cutting Line and two bias strips 1" X 4-1/2" for sleeve binding.

Assemble sleeves according to Basic Instructions for Puffed Sleeve with Narrow Binding. Attach sleeves to bodice and then sew underarm sleeves according to Basic Instructions.

SKIRT

Cut a rectangle 11-1/2" X 45". Sew center back seam and hem skirt bottom as directed in Basic Instructions.

Nina (lower right) and
family in the '30s

Embroidery Design

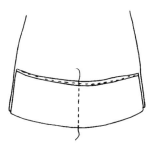

Apron Pockets

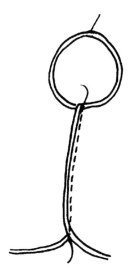

Underarm Seams of Apron

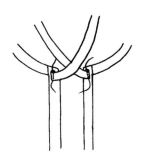

Sewing Ties to Back of Apron

Gather and attach the skirt according to Basic Instructions #10. Lapping right back over left back, sew two snaps to dress bodice.

APRON WITH POCKETS

Trace apron front pattern piece outline and center embroidery design onto the outlined apron. DO NOT CUT OUT YET. Put fabric into 4"-5" embroidery hoop.

Using two strands of embroidery floss and a #7 or 8 crewel needle, work the design as follows: cherries--red, leaves--green, stems--brown. All are done with outline stitch, except short straight stitches for the shading of the cherries.

Remove fabric from hoop and iron on the wrong side, using a towel underneath so as not to flatten the stitching.

Cut out apron front and two backs, plus one pocket.

Right sides together, sew the front to the backs at the shoulders.

Press the bias tape in half lengthwise. Enclose the top edge of the pocket in bias tape and stitch close to the edge of the tape. Place the unfinished edge of the pocket flush with the lower front apron edge, wrong side of pocket to right side of apron front. Stitch vertical lines through the pocket and apron as shown on the pocket pattern piece.

Enclose all remaining unfinished edges of the apron in bias tape (armholes, neck, back, sides and lower edges) and stitch as you did across the top of the pocket.

Sew underarm seams by lapping the apron front over the side edges of the apron backs and stitching over the previous stitching on the bias tape.

For apron ties, cut two pieces of bias tape 10-1/2" long. Press it in half lengthwise and stitch along edges, tucking in short ends of the tape to enclose them in the stitching. Sew to center backs just below the neck binding and at right angles to the center back opening.

WHAT TO DO FOR OTHER DOLLS

All dolls use the Short or Medium Sleeve pattern with Cuff Cutting Line.

(The apron is exactly the same except for different size pattern pieces.)

Shirley: Sleeve bias bindings are 1" X 4". The skirt is 6" X 30".
Violet: Sleeve bias bindings are 1" X 4-1/4". The skirt is 5-3/4" X 34".
Götz/Pleasant Co.: Sleeve bias bindings are 1" X 5". The skirt is 7-1/4" X 38".
Hilary/T.J. 501: Sleeve bias bindings are 1" X 4". The skirt is 7" X 40".
Jenny/Emily: Sleeve bias bindings are 1" X 4-1/4". The skirt is 8-3/4" X 45".
Angel/May/Seeley ALB9873/MB140S 14": Sleeve bias bindings are 1" X 4-1/4". The skirt is 7-3/4" X 40".
Christina/T.J. 512: Sleeve bias bindings are 1" X 4". The skirt is 7-3/4" X 40".
Elise/Georgia: Sleeve bias bindings are 1" X 4-1/2". The skirt is 8-3/4" X 40".
Shay: Sleeve bias bindings are 1" X 5-1/4". The skirt is 8-3/4" X 45".

Tiffany: Sleeve bias bindings are 1" X 5". The skirt is 9" X 45".
Heidi: Sleeve bias bindings are 1" X 5-3/4". The skirt is 9" X 45".

Jenny's Flour Sack Dress and Kitty Face Apron

(Jenny's body is from the pattern provided by the mold company.)

<u>Supplies:</u>

2/3 yd. calico fabric
1/3 yd. elastic 1/8" wide
1/4 yd. white broadcloth for apron
1 package single fold bias tape
Light gray, dark gray, blue and pink embroidery floss
3 small snaps

BODICE

Cut out two fronts and four backs using Yoke Dress bodice pieces. Assemble bodice according to Basic Instructions

Cut out two sleeves using Medium Sleeve pattern piece with Elastic Finish Cutting Line.

Assemble sleeves according to Basic Instructions for Elastic Sleeve Bottom with Ruffle, using 3-3/4" elastic for each sleeve. Attach sleeves to bodice and then sew underarm sleeves according to Basic Instructions.

SKIRT

Cut a rectangle 8-3/4" X 45". Sew center back seam and hem skirt bottom as directed in Basic Instructions.

Gather and attach the skirt according to Basic Instructions #10. Lapping right back over left back, sew two snaps to dress bodice.

KITTY FACE APRON

Trace apron front pattern piece outline and center embroidery design onto outlined apron. DO NOT CUT OUT YET. Put fabric into 4"-5" embroidery hoop.

Embroidery Design

Using two strands of embroidery floss and a #7 or 8 crewel needle, work the design as follows: Eye centers--blue satin stitches, eye outlines--pale gray outline stitches plus straight stitches for eyelashes, nose and tongue--pink short satin stitches, mouth--pale gray outline stitches, whiskers--dark gray outline stitches.

Remove fabric from hoop and iron on the wrong side, using a towel underneath so as not to flatten the stitching.

Cut out apron front and two backs.

Right sides together, sew the front to the backs at the sides only.

Press the bias tape in half lengthwise. Enclose neck and armhole edges of the apron (skipping the shoulder seam edges) in the bias tape and stitch close to the edge of the tape. Enclose the center back and lower edges of the apron in bias tape, tucking in 1/4" on the short ends of the tape at the back neck so all raw edges are enclosed. Stitch. Sew one snap at back neck.

WHAT TO DO FOR OTHER DOLLS

(The apron is exactly the same except for different size pattern pieces.)

All dolls use the Short or Medium Sleeve pattern with Elastic Finish Cutting Line.

Shirley: 3-1/2" elastic for each sleeve. The skirt is 6" X 30".
Violet: 3-1/4" elastic for each sleeve. The skirt is 5-3/4" X 34".
Götz/Pleasant Co.: 4-1/4" elastic for each sleeve. The skirt is 7-1/4" X 38".
Hilary/T.J. 501: 3-1/2" elastic for each sleeve. The skirt is 7" X 40".
Emily: Follow Jenny's instructions exactly.
Angel/May/Seeley ALB9873/MB140S 14": 3-3/4" elastic for each sleeve. The skirt is 7-3/4" X 40".
Christina/T.J. 512: 3-1/4" elastic for each sleeve. The skirt is 7-3/4" X 40".
Elise/Georgia: 3-1/2" elastic for each sleeve. The skirt is 8-3/4" X 40".
Shay: 4" elastic for each sleeve. The skirt is 8-3/4" X 45".
Tiffany: 4-1/4" elastic for each sleeve. The skirt is 9" X 45".
Willow: 3-1/4" elastic for each sleeve. The skirt is 11-1/2" X 45".
Heidi: 5" elastic for each sleeve. The skirt is 9" X 45".

Emily's Ruffled Dress

(Emily's body is from the pattern provided by the mold company.)

<u>Supplies:</u>

2/3 yd. dotted Swiss fabric
4 yd. pre-gathered lace 1" wide (smaller dolls use 5/8" wide)
1/2 yd. white ribbon 1/4" wide
1/2 yd. pre-gathered lace edging 3/8" wide
1 yd. white ribbon for belt 1/2" wide
2 small snaps

BODICE

Cut out two fronts and four backs using Square-Necked Waist Dress Bodice pattern. Assemble bodice according to Basic Instructions.

Place the 1/4" wide ribbon so that it frames the square neckline, folding under each end of the ribbon 1/4" so that the raw edges are tucked in, and having one edge of the ribbon flush with the fabric neckline. You must miter the corners. Sew ribbon to bodice by stitching very close to the neckline. Place the 3/8" wide pre-gathered lace edging around the neckline, mitering corners, and tuck the heading of it underneath the ribbon edge so it is just barely covered. Stitch on top of the ribbon close to the edge, being sure you are catching the lace at the same time.

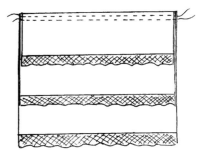

Applying Lace to Neckline

SLEEVES

Cut out two sleeves using the Medium Sleeve pattern piece with Cuff Cutting Line. Cut two bias bindings 1" X 4-1/2". Assemble sleeves according to Basic Instructions for Puffed Sleeve with Narrow Binding. Attach sleeves to bodice and then sew underarm sleeves according to Basic Instructions.

SKIRT

Cut three strips of fabric on grain for the ruffles: 6-1/2" X 45"; 4-1/2" X 45"; and 2-1/2" X 45".

Cut the 1" wide lace edging into three pieces to match the lengths of the ruffles. For each of the three ruffles, press one long edge under 1/4". Place the heading of the lace underneath the folded edge of the fabric (both fabric and lace are right sides up) and stitch close to the folded edge of the fabric.

Layer the three ruffles by stacking them, all right sides up, with widest ruffle on the bottom and the narrowest ruffle on the top. The raw edges on top and sides should be flush. From now on you will treat the layered ruffles as one unit.

Sew center back seam and placket as directed in Basic Instructions, keeping ruffles and their lace edging matched up. This requires careful pinning. There is, of course, no bottom hem.

Gather the top edge of the skirt and attach it to the bodice according to Basic Instructions #10.

Lapping right back over left back, sew two snaps to dress bodice.

Cut a 12" length from the 1/2" wide ribbon and tie a bow. Tack it to the center of the rest of the ribbon. Tie the ribbon around the waist of the dress with the bow in front. Notch all four ends of the ribbon.

WHAT TO DO FOR OTHER DOLLS

NOTE: The following dolls require 5/8" wide pre-gathered lace for the skirt ruffles instead of 1" wide, for better proportion: *Shirley, Violet, Götz/Pleasant Co., Hilary/T.J. 18", Angel/May/Seeley ALB9873/MB140S 14" compo, Christina/T.J. 20"*. The rest all can use 1" wide lace. Also, the dolls using 30" long ruffles only require 2-1/2 yd. rather than nearly 4 yd.

All dolls use the Short or Medium Sleeve pattern with Cuff Cutting Line.

Shirley: Sleeve bias bindings are 1" X 4". The skirt ruffles are: 4-1/4" X 30";

Gathering the
Layered Skirt Ruffles

2-3/4" X 30"; and 1-1/4" X 30".

Violet: Sleeve bias bindings are 1" X 4-1/4". The skirt ruffles are: 4-3/4" X 40"; 3" X 40"; and 1-1/2" X 40".

Götz/Pleasant Co.: Sleeve bias bindings are 1" X 5". The skirt ruffles are: 5-1/2" X 45"; 3-3/4" X 45"; and 2-1/4" X 45".

Hilary/T.J. 501/Christina/T.J. 512: Sleeve bias bindings are 1" X 4". The skirt ruffles are: 5-3/4" X 45"; 4" X 45"; and 2-1/4" X 45".

Jenny: Follow Emily's instructions exactly.

Angel/May/Seeley ALB9873/MB140S 14": Sleeve bias bindings are 1" X 4-1/4". The skirt ruffles are: 5-3/4" X 45"; 4" X 45"; and 2-1/4" X 45".

Elise/Georgia: Sleeve bias bindings are 1" X 4-1/2". The skirt ruffles are: 7" X 45"; 4-3/4" X 45"; and 2-1/2" x 45".

Shay: Sleeve bias bindings are 1" X 5-1/4". The skirt ruffles are: 7" X 45"; 4-3/4" X 45"; and 2-1/2" X 45".

Tiffany: Sleeve bias bindings are 1" X 5". The skirt ruffles are: 7-1/2" X 45"; 5" X 45"; and 2-3/4" X 45".

Willow: Sleeve bias bindings are 1" X 4-1/2". The skirt ruffles are: 9-1/4" X 45"; 6-1/4" X 45"; and 3-1/4" X 45".

Heidi: Sleeve bias bindings are 1" X 5-3/4". The skirt ruffles are: 6-1/2" X 45"; 4-1/2" X 45"; and 2-1/2" X 45".

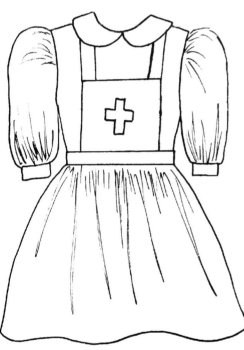

Georgia's Nurse Uniform

(Georgia's body is from the pattern provided by the mold company.)

Supplies:

1/4 yd. light blue broadcloth
1/2 yd. white broadcloth
1/4 yd. red poplin
1/4 yd. navy blue poplin
9" navy blue single fold bias tape
Scraps of red felt
Scrap of heavy weight non-woven interfacing
7 small snaps

Large Cross

BLOUSE

This blouse opens down the back.

Cut out two fronts and four backs from light blue broadcloth, using the Back Opening Blouse pattern pieces. Assemble bodice and bodice lining according to Basic Instructions, but do not sew lining to bodice yet.

Cut out four Small Peter Pan Collar pieces from the white broadcloth as indicated on the pattern and assemble according to Basic Instructions for Peter Pan Collars.

Right sides together, sew lining to bodice, sandwiching collar between them, stitching up the center backs and around the neckline, just as you would normally sew the bodice together even if there were no collar there.

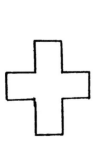

Small Cross

Cut out two sleeves from the light blue broadcloth using Medium Sleeve pattern piece with Cuff Cutting Line. From the white broadcloth cut two on-grain strips 2" X 4-1/4" for cuff.

Assemble sleeves according to Basic Instructions for Gathered Sleeve with Cuff. Attach sleeves to bodice and then sew underarm sleeves according to Basic Instructions.

Zig-zag or serge lower edge of blouse to finish. Lapping right back over left back, sew three snaps to the center back opening, spacing them evenly.

APRON

From white broadcloth, cut out the skirt: 8-1/4" X 45"; the waistband: 2" X 12"; bib and bib lining: 3" X 3-1/2" each; and two straps: 1-1/4" X 8-1/2" each.

Narrow hem both long edges and one short end of each of the straps.

Baste the unhemmed ends of the straps to one of the 3" edges of the bib, right sides together. Sew bib lining to bib, sandwiching the straps in between. Stitch around the three sides of the bib as shown, being careful not to catch the straps in the side seams. Trim seam allowances, turn right side out and press.

Sew center back seam and hem skirt bottom as directed in Basic Instructions.

Gather top of skirt to fit waistband. Pin the wrong side of the skirt to the right side of the waistband, with the waistband extending 1/4" beyond the skirt. Stitch in place. Press the remaining long edge of the waistband 1/4" toward the wrong side. Tucking in the short ends of the waistband, fold the waistband over to the right side and topstitch all three sides.

Pin bib to center of apron, with unfinished edge of bib slightly below the waistband seam. Stitch over the waistband seam to secure bib. Lapping right over left 1/4", sew a snap to the waistband.

Sew one-half of a snap to the back waistband 1" to the left and right of the center back. Try the apron on the doll, crossing the bib straps in back, and mark the straps where the other half of the snaps should be. Sew them in place.

Cut a cross from the red felt and glue to center of bib with fabric glue.

CAPE

Cut two capes from the navy blue fabric and two cape linings from the red fabric. Right sides together, sew darts in each of the four pieces.

Right sides together, sew center back seams of navy cape and then of red lining. Press. Right sides together, sew navy cape to red cape lining, stitching around the sides and across the bottom. Leave the top open.

Trim seam allowances and turn right side out. Press. Treating the cape and its

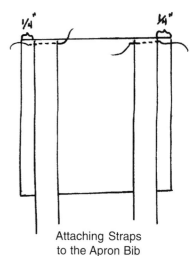

Attaching Straps
to the Apron Bib

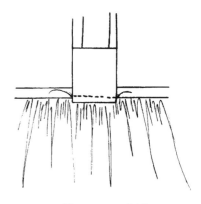

Waistband to Skirt

Placement of Bib
on Apron Skirt

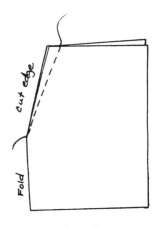

Cape Darts

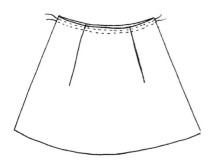

Gathering Cape and
Lining as One Unit

Bias Tape to Cape Neckline

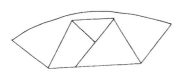

Back View of
Nurse's Cap

lining as one unit, gather the top unfinished edge of the cape. Pull the gathering threads so that the top measures 6-3/4" across.

Center the gathered cape on the navy bias tape. Pin the right side of the tape to the red lining side of the cape. Stitch in place. Fold bias tape over to the navy side of the cape and pin in place. Tucking in the short ends of the bias tape 1/4" so they don't fray over time, stitch from one end of the bias tape to the other, enclosing the top of the cape.

Sew a snap 1/2" from the ends of the bias tape so that when the cape is worn, the tape crosses and snaps just above the apron's bib.

NURSE'S CAP

Cut one cap from the heavy interfacing. Fold the brim along the fold line marked on pattern. Pull the left side of the pointed section on the back to overlap the square section to make a right angle. Repeat with the right side. Tack all sections together or glue. Cut a small cross from the red felt and glue to the center of the brim.

WHAT TO DO FOR OTHER DOLLS

The capes are all the same size unless you wish change the length, a matter of personal preference. Nurse capes for dolls frequently ranged from a very short capelet size to below skirt hem length. Feel free to make a design decision yourself!

The nurse's cap is a one-size-fits-all, within reason. Before you sew the flaps in, pin it in place and try it on the doll. Wigs can make a big difference, so you may want to make it tighter or more loose and then stitch it together.

All dolls use the Short or Medium Sleeve pattern with Cuff Cutting Line.

Shirley: Sleeve cuffs are 1-1/2" X 4". The apron skirt is: 5-1/2" X 30"; the waistband: 1-1/2" X 10-1/2"; bib and bib lining: 3" X 3" each; and the straps are: 1-1/4" X 7" each.
Violet: Sleeve cuffs are 1-1/2" X 4-1/4". The apron skirt is 5-3/4" X 38"; the waistband: 1-1/2" X 11-1/2"; bib and bib lining: 3" X 3" each; and the straps are: 1-1/4" X 7" each.
Götz/Pleasant Co.: Sleeve cuffs are 1-1/2" X 5". The apron skirt is 6-1/4" X 45"; the waistband: 2" X 12-1/2"; bib and bib lining: 3" X 3-1/2"; and the straps are: 1-1/4" X 8" each.
Hilary/T.J. 501: Sleeve cuffs are 1-1/2" X 4". The apron skirt is 6-1/2" X 45"; the waistband: 2" X 11-1/2"; bib and bib lining: 3" X 3-1/2"; and the straps are: 1-1/4" X 7-1/2" each.
Jenny/Emily: Sleeve cuffs are 2" X 4-1/4". The apron skirt is 7-1/2" X 45"; the waistband: 2" X 13-3/4"; bib and bib lining: 3-1/2" X 3-1/2"; and the straps are: 1-1/4" X 8-1/2" each.
Angel/May/Seeley ALB9873/MB140S 14": Sleeve cuffs are 2" X 4-1/4". The apron skirt is 7" X 45"; the waistband: 2" X 11"; bib and bib lining 3" X 3-1/2"; and the straps are 1-1/4" X 8" each.
Christina/T.J. 512: Sleeve cuffs are 1-1/2" X 4". The apron skirt is 7" X 45"; the waistband: 2" X 11"; bib and bib lining: 3" X 3-1/2"; and the straps are: 1-1/4" X 7-1/2" each.

Elise: Follow Georgia's instructions exactly.

Shay: Sleeve cuffs are 2" X 5-1/4". The apron skirt is 7-1/2" X 45"; the waistband: 2" X 11-1/4"; bib and bib lining: 3-1/2" X 3-1/2"; and the straps are: 1-1/4" X 8" each.

Tiffany: Sleeve cuffs are 2" X 5". The apron skirt is 8-1/4" X 45"; the waistband: 2" X 11"; bib and bib lining: 3-1/2" X 3-1/2"; and the straps are: 1-1/4" X 9" each.

Willow: Sleeve cuffs are 2" X 5-3/4". The apron skirt is 10" X 45"; the waistband 2" X 12-3/4"; bib and bib lining: 4" wide and 3-1/2" tall; and the straps are: 1-1/4" X 12".

Heidi: Sleeve cuffs are 2" X 5-3/4". The apron skirt is 7-1/4" X 30"; the waistband: 2" X 15-3/4"; bib and bib lining: 4" wide and 3-1/2" tall; and the straps are: 1-1/4" X 10" each.

Christina's Sailor Dress

(Christina's body is the T.J. 512 porcelain.)

<u>Supplies:</u>

1/2 yd. nautical or patriotic print fabric
Scrap of red broadcloth for scarf and cuffs
2 snaps

BODICE

Cut out two fronts and four backs from nautical or patriotic print fabric, using Yoke Dress bodice pieces. Assemble bodice according to Basic Instructions.

Cut out two sleeves from nautical/patriotic print, using Short Sleeve pattern piece with Cuff Cutting Line. Cut out two on-grain cuffs from the red fabric measuring 1-1/2" X 4".

Assemble sleeves according to Basic Instructions for Gathered Sleeve with Cuff. Attach sleeves to bodice and then sew underarm sleeves according to Basic Instructions.

SKIRT

Cut a rectangle 8-1/4" X 38". Sew center back seam and hem skirt bottom as directed in Basic Instructions.

Gather and attach the skirt according to Basic Instructions, #10.

Lapping right back over left back, sew two snaps to dress bodice.

SAILOR SCARF

Cut scarf and scarf lining from red fabric, using appropriate pattern piece. Right sides together, stitch all around the scarf except for the back straight edge. Leave that open so you can turn it. Trim away seam allowances, turn

Joyce in sailor dress, 1946

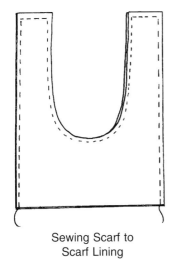

Sewing Scarf to
Scarf Lining

right side out and press. Top stitch all around the scarf so that the open end is closed. Tie around neck of doll.

This scarf can be jazzed up by sewing middy braid (or soutache) 1/4" from the edge along the three straight sides. Small metallic stars or embroidered anchor motifs can be glued to the corners at the back of the scarf.

WHAT TO DO FOR OTHER DOLLS

All dolls use Short or Medium Sleeve pattern with Cuff Cutting Line.

Shirley: Sleeve cuffs are 1-1/2" X 4". The skirt is: 6" X 30".
Violet: Sleeve cuffs are 1-1/2" X 4-1/4". The skirt is 5-3/4" X 34".
Götz/Pleasant Co.: Sleeve cuffs are 1-1/2" X 5". The skirt is 7-1/4" X 38".
Hilary/T.J. 501: Sleeve cuffs are 1-1/2" X 4". The skirt is 7-1/4" X 38".
Jenny/Emily: Sleeve cuffs are 2" X 4-1/4". The skirt is 8-3/4" X 45".
Angel/May/Seeley ALB9873/MB140S 14": Sleeve cuffs are 2" X 4-1/4". The skirt is 7-3/4" X 40".
Elise/Georgia: Sleeve cuffs are 1-1/2" X 4-1/2". The skirt is 8-3/4" X 40".
Shay: Sleeve cuffs are 2" X 5-1/4". The skirt is 8-3/4" X 45".
Tiffany: Sleeve cuffs are 2" X 5". The skirt is 9" X 45".
Willow: Sleeve cuffs are 2" X 5-3/4". The skirt is 11-1/2" X 45".
Heidi: Sleeve cuffs are 2" X 5-3/4". The skirt is 9" X 45".

Heidi's Heart Bib Pinafore and Plain Sleeved Dress

(Heidi's body is from the pattern provided by the mold company.)

<u>Supplies:</u>

2/3 yd. fabric for dress
1/2 yd. white broadcloth for pinafore, collar and cuffs
3-1/4 yd. flat eyelet lace edging 1" wide
    (smaller dolls require less lace, and only 1/2"-3/4" wide)
4 small snaps

DRESS BODICE

Cut out two fronts and four backs using Waist Dress bodice pieces. Assemble bodice and bodice lining according to Basic Instructions, but do not sew lining to bodice yet.

Cut out four Small Peter Pan Collar pieces from the white broadcloth as indicated on the pattern and assemble according to Basic Instructions for Peter Pan Collars.

Place collar on the right side of the bodice as shown and baste to bodice neckline.

Right sides together, sew lining to bodice, sandwiching collar between them, stitching up the center backs and around the neckline, just as you would normally sew the bodice together even if there were no collar there. Do not sew side seams yet.

Cuff to Cuff Lining

Cut out two sleeves from dress fabric, using Short Straight Sleeve pattern piece with Cuff Cutting Line.

Cut out four cuff pieces from white broadcloth, using the Pointed Cuff pattern piece. Right sides together, sew each cuff to a cuff lining, stitching along the pointed edge only. Trim seam allowances, turn right side out and press.

Sew the long unfinished edge of each lined cuff to the bottom edge of the wrong side of each sleeve. Fold cuff out to the right side of the sleeve and press.

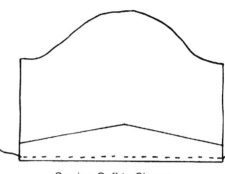

Sewing Cuff to Sleeve

These sleeves are straight and only eased, not gathered, at the cap. Right sides together, sew the sleeves to the bodice armholes. Then sew the underarm seams from cuff to waist.

SKIRT

WARNING: This skirt is short short! The dimensions given for skirts are the shortest possible for the dolls listed. If in doubt, measure first. See the section under Hems in the Basic Instructions regarding skirt lengths appropriate for different types of dolls.

Cut a rectangle 7-1/2" X 45". Sew center back seam and hem skirt bottom as directed in Basic Instructions.

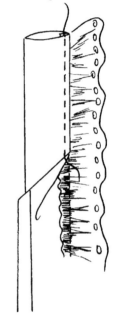

Enclosing Eyelet Lace in Strap

Gather and attach the skirt according to Basic Instructions #10. Lapping right back over left back, sew three snaps to dress bodice.

HEART BIB PINAFORE

From white broadcloth cut out two yokes, using Heart Bib pattern piece. Cut out two straps 2" X 8-1/2" each.

Cut a piece of the eyelet lace 17" long and gather it. Fold both the long edges of one of the straps toward the wrong side 1/4". Then fold the strap in half lengthwise and press. Pull the gathering threads on the eyelet lace so that it fits the strap. Enclose the gathered edge of the eyelet lace in the strap so that the strap just barely covers the gathering threads of the lace. Top stitch along the folded edge of the fabric where it meets the eyelet lace. Repeat for second strap.

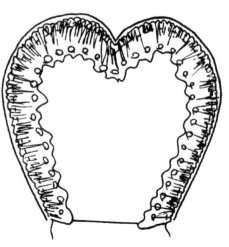

Applying Gathered Eyelet
to Heart Bib

Cut a 20" piece of eyelet lace and gather it. Right sides together, pin the gathered eyelet around the curved edges of the heart bib and stitch. Right sides together, pin the bib lining to the bib, sandwiching the gathered eyelet inside. Stitch around the curved edges of the bib. (This is the same principle as putting a ruffle around a pillow.) Trim the seam allowance, turn right side out and press the bib--not the eyelet.

To make the pinafore's skirt, cut a rectangle from the white broadcloth 5" X

Sewing Waistband to Pinafore Skirt

Sewiwng Bib to Pinafore Skirt

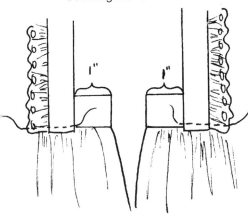

Attaching Straps to Back of Pinafore

45". Cut a waistband on grain 2" X 15-3/4". Press one long edge of the skirt under 1/4". Place the remaining ungathered eyelet lace underneath the folded skirt fabric and top stitch.

Hem the center back edges of the pinafore's skirt. Gather the top of the pinafore's skirt to fit the waistband, with the waistband extending beyond the skirt 1/4" on each end. Sew right side of waistband to wrong side of skirt. Press the remaining long edge of the waistband 1/4" toward the wrong side and fold the waistband over to the right side, tucking in the short ends of the waistband. Top stitch close to the fold, enclosing the skirt gathers.

Place bib in center of pinafore's skirt so that the straight bottom edge of the bib extends slightly below the waistband stitching. Sew to waistband over previous stitching.

Lapping right over left, check the pinafore's fit around the doll's waist and sew a snap to the pinafore waistband. Position the straps on the waistband approximately 1" on either side of the center back. Stitch straps in place.

Position the straps underneath the bib front where shown on the pattern piece, extending the strap 3/4" below the bib's top seam. Mark for placement of snaps and sew them on. If you wish you can sew decorative buttons on the front of the bib to cover the snap stitches.

WHAT TO DO FOR OTHER DOLLS

All dolls can use the Short Straight Sleeve pattern piece for their size.

Shirley: The dress skirt is: 5-1/2" X 30". The pinafore skirt is: 3-1/2" X 30"; waistband: 1-1/2" X 10-1/2"; straps: 1-1/4" X 7" each. Use narrower eyelet lace, 30" for pinafore, 16" for bib, 14" for each strap.

Violet: The dress skirt is 5-3/4" X 38". The pinafore skirt is: 3-3/4" X 38"; waistband: 1-1/2" X 11-1/2"; straps: 1-1/4" X 7" each. Use narrower eyelet lace, 38" for pinafore, 16" for bib, 14" for each strap.

Götz/Pleasant Co.: The dress skirt is: 6-1/4" X 45". The pinafore skirt is: 3-3/4" X 45"; waistband: 2" X 12-1/2"; straps are 2" X 7-3/4" each. 1" wide eyelet required for pinafore: 45"; for bib: 18"; and for straps: 15-1/2" each.

Hilary/T.J. 501: The dress skirt is: 6-1/2" X 45". The pinafore skirt is: 3-3/4" X 45"; waistband: 2" X 11-1/2"; straps are 2" X 7-1/2" each. 1" wide eyelet required for pinafore: 45"; for bib: 18"; and for straps: 15" each.

Christina/T.J. 512: The dress skirt is 7" X 45". The pinafore skirt is: 4-1/4" X 45"; waistband: 2" X 11-1/2"; straps are 2" X 7-1/2" each. 1" wide eyelet required for pinafore: 45"; for bib: 18"; and for straps: 15" each.

Jenny/Emily: The dress skirt is 7-1/4" X 45". The pinafore skirt is: 4-1/2" X 45"; waistband: 2" X 13-3/4"; straps are 2" X 7-1/2" each. 1" wide eyelet required for pinafore: 45"; for bib: 18"; and for straps: 15" each.

Angel/May/Seeley ALB9873/MB140S 14": The dress skirt is 6-1/2" X 45". The pinafore skirt is: 3-3/4" X 45"; waistband: 2" X 11"; straps are 2" X 8" each. 1" wide eyelet required for pinafore: 45"; for bib: 18"; and for straps: 16" each.

Elise/Georgia: The dress skirt is 7-3/4" X 45". The pinafore skirt is: 5" X 45"; waistband: 2" X 12"; straps are 2" X 8" each. 1" wide eyelet required for pinafore: 45"; for bib: 18"; and for straps: 16" each.

Shay: The dress skirt is 7-1/2" X 45". The pinafore skirt is: 4-3/4" X 45";

waistband: 2" X 11-1/4"; straps are 2" X 8" each. 1" wide eyelet required for pinafore: 45"; for bib: 20"; and for straps: 17" each.

Tiffany: The dress skirt is 8-1/4" X 45". The pinafore skirt is: 5-1/2" X 45; waistband: 2" X 11"; straps are 2" X 9" each. 1" wide eyelet required for pinafore: 45"; for bib: 20"; and for straps: 18" each.

Willow: The dress skirt is 10" X 45". The pinafore skirt is: 7-1/4" X 45"; waistband: 2" X 12-3/4"; straps are 2" X 12". 1" wide eyelet required for pinafore: 45"; for bib: 20"; and for straps: 24" each.

Hannah's Teapot Pinafore and Yoke Dress

(Hannah is an 18" vinyl Götz doll with non-articulated shoulder and hip joints, the same cloth body as that of Anne--last doll in the first page of naked doll photos. Compare Anne's body to the one next to her, redheaded Ginger. Ginger's body is identical to the Pleasant Company's American Girl dolls, also manufactured by Götz Dolls. Articulated joints or not, these dolls share the same measurements and pattern pieces.)

Supplies:

1/2 yd. teapot print fabric for pinafore
2/3 yd. solid fabric for dress
5 small snaps

YOKE DRESS BODICE

Cut out two fronts and four backs, using the Yoke Dress bodice pieces. Assemble bodice and bodice lining according to Basic Instructions.

Cut out two sleeves using Short Sleeve pattern piece with Cuff Cutting Line and two bias strips 1" X 5" for sleeve binding.

Assemble sleeves according to Basic Instructions for Puffed Sleeve with Narrow Binding. Attach sleeves to bodice and then sew underarm sleeves according to Basic Instructions.

SKIRT

Cut a rectangle 7-1/4" X 45". Sew center back seam and hem skirt bottom as directed in Basic Instructions.

Gather and attach the skirt according to Basic Instructions #10. Lapping right back over left back, sew two snaps to dress bodice.

PINAFORE YOKE

Cut out two pinafore fronts and four pinafore backs from teapot print fabric, using Teapot Pinafore Yoke pattern pieces. Cut out two Teapot Pinafore Ruffles from pattern piece, and two ties, each 2" X 18".

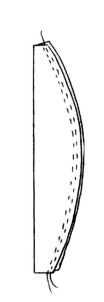

Gathering Pinafore Ruffle

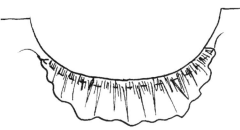

Applying Ruffle to
Pinafore Armhole

Sew shoulder seams of pinafore yoke and pinafore yoke lining as you would in the beginning of Basic Instructions for bodices/yokes. Right sides together, sew pinafore yoke to yoke lining, stitching center backs and around neckline. Trim seam allowances, turn right side out and press.

Fold each pinafore ruffle lengthwise, right sides out. Press. Gather the curved edges of each ruffle. Pull gathering threads of ruffle so that the ruffle fits between *'s on each armhole. Stitch ruffle to pinafore yoke only (not yoke lining).

Press armhole edges of pinafore yoke and yoke lining 1/4" toward wrong side. Pin pinafore yoke to pinafore yoke lining all along the armhole edge, enclosing the ruffle seam allowance within. Slip stitch all around the armhole edge on the inside of the garment.

Leave the side seams undone for the moment.

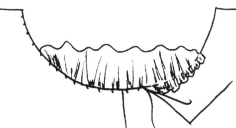

Slipstitch Lining to Pinafore

PINAFORE TIES

Narrow hem both long edges of each tie. On one end of each tie, fold the fabric, right sides together, at a 45 degree angle so that the end meets the long edge. Stitch. Turn to right side and press.

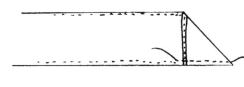

Pinafore Tie

Make a small pleat in the remaining short end of the tie so that it fits the underarm seam of the pinafore yoke. 1/4" of the bodice must extend below the tie so that when you sew the bodice to the skirt, the tie will hang free.

Pin the pleated end, right sides together, to the underarm seam of the front pinafore yoke, so that the tie ends at least 1/4" above the bottom edge of the yoke. Pin the pinafore front yoke to the back yokes, enclosing the pleated ends of the ties, and stitch the side seams of the pinafore yoke.

PINAFORE SKIRT

Cut a rectangle 6-1/4" X 45". Sew center back seam and hem skirt bottom as directed in Basic Instructions.

Gather and attach the skirt to the yoke according to Basic Instructions #10. Lapping right back over left back, sew two snaps to pinafore yoke.

WHAT TO DO FOR OTHER DOLLS

All dolls use the Short or Medium Sleeve pattern with Cuff Cutting Line.

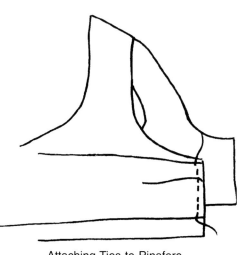

Attaching Ties to Pinafore

Shirley: Sleeve bias bindings are 1" X 4". The skirt is 6" X 30". The pinafore skirt is 5" X 30" and the ties are 1-1/2" X 14".
Violet: Sleeve bias bindings are 1" X 4-1/4". The skirt is 5-3/4" X 40". The pinafore skirt is 4-3/4" X 40" and the ties are 1-1/2" X 14".
Hilary/T.J. 501: Sleeve bias bindings are 1" X 4". The skirt is 7" X 45". The pinafore skirt is 6" X 45" and the ties are 2" X 18".
Christina/T.J. 512: Sleeve bias bindings are 1" X 4". The skirt is 7-3/4" X 45. The pinafore skirt is 6-3/4" X 45" and the ties are 2" X 18".
Jenny/Emily: Sleeve bias bindings are 1" X 4-1/4". The skirt is 8-3/4" X 45".

The pinafore skirt is 7-3/4" X 45" and the ties are 2" X 18".

Angel/May/Seeley ALB9873/MB140S 14": Sleeve bias bindings are 1" X 4-1/4". The skirt is 7-3/4" X 45". The pinafore skirt is 6-3/4" X 45" and the ties are 2" X 18".

Elise/Georgia: Sleeve bias bindings are 1" X 4-1/2". The skirt is 8-3/4" X 45". The pinafore skirt is 7-3/4" X 45" and the ties are 2" X 18".

Shay: Sleeve bias bindings are 1" X 5-1/4". The skirt is 8-3/4" X 45". The pinafore skirt is 7-3/4" X 45" and the ties are 2" X 18".

Tiffany: Sleeve bias bindings are 1" X 5". The skirt is 9" X 45". The pinafore skirt is 8" X 45" and the ties are 2" X 18".

Willow: 2/3 yd. dress fabric required. Sleeve bias bindings are 1" X 4-1/2". The skirt is 11-1/2" X 45". The pinafore skirt is 10-1/2" X 45" and the ties are 2" X 18".

Heidi: Sleeve bias bindings are 1" X 5-3/4". The skirt is 9" X 45". The pinafore skirt is 8" X 45" and the ties are 2" X 21".

Angel's White and Red Dotted Dress

(Angel's body is from Seeley's porcelain MB ALB9873 mold.)

<u>Supplies:</u>

2/3 yd. dotted nylon organdy
2/3 yd. white taffeta for underlining
Scrap of white nylon for collar
1 yd. picot edge ribbon, 1/2" wide
3 small snaps

BODICE

Cut out one front and two backs from dotted nylon organdy, and one front and two backs from white taffeta, using Waist Dress bodice pieces. Assemble bodice and bodice lining according to Basic Instructions, but do not sew lining to bodice yet.

Cut out four Small Peter Pan Collar pieces from the white nylon as indicated on the pattern and assemble according to Basic Instructions for Peter Pan Collars.

Place collar on the right side of the bodice as shown and baste to bodice neckline.

Right sides together, sew lining to bodice, sandwiching collar between them, stitching up the center backs and around the neckline, just as you would normally sew the bodice together even if there were no collar there.

Cut out two sleeves from dotted nylon organdy, using Short Sleeve pattern piece with Cuff Cutting Line and two bias strips 1" X 4-1/4" for sleeve binding.

Assemble sleeves according to Basic Instructions for Puffed Sleeve with Narrow Binding. Attach sleeves to bodice and then sew underarm sleeves

Jean in tiered dress, 1955

46

Top tier

middle tier

Bottom tier

Hemmed edge

Skirt Construction

From a Simplicity Pattern

Joan, Jenny, Cousin Linda,
With Grandpa, 1955

according to Basic Instructions.

SKIRT

This skirt has three gathered tiers, and each tier is constructed with a taffeta underlining so that the skirt sticks out without use of a can-can.

(You remember those scratchy things, don't you? If you really want to be authentic, go ahead and make the skirt simply from organdy and make a separate can-can as follows: Using stiff netting, cut out the three tiers, but add 1/2" to the width of the top tier and decrease the width of the bottom tier by 1/2". Sew the three parts together as you would the skirt, but fold the raw edge of the top tier under 3/8", sew a casing and run 1/4" elastic through it to fit around your doll's waist. To finish off the bottom tier, sew white or pastel 1/4" wide ribbon to the bottom edge, stitching along both edges of the ribbon.)

Cut three sections of dotted nylon organdy and three of the taffeta underlining. The tiers for Angel/May measure as follows: 1-1/2" X 20"; 2" X 32"; and 3" X 55" (this section will have to be pieced).

Narrow hem one long edge of the longest dotted nylon organdy tier and the longest taffeta tier.

Pin each dotted nylon organdy tier to its respective taffeta underlining, wrong side of the dotted Swiss to the right side of the taffeta. From this point on, treat the underlined sections each as one unit.

Run gathering stitches along the long, unhemmed edge of the longest tier, one long edge of the medium tier and one long edge of the shortest tier. Remember that you are treating the dotted nylon organdy and its taffeta underlining as one unit.

Pull the gathering threads of the medium tier to fit the ungathered long edge of the shortest tier, right sides together. Stitch. Pull the gathering threads of the longest tier to fit the ungathered long edge of the medium tier, right sides together. Stitch.

Sew center back seam and placket as directed in Basic Instructions, keeping tiers matched up. This requires careful pinning. There is, of course, no bottom hem.

Gather the top edge of the skirt and attach it to the bodice according to Basic Instructions #10.

Lapping right back over left back, sew three snaps to dress bodice.

Tie the ribbon around the waist of the dress with the bow in back.

WHAT TO DO FOR OTHER DOLLS

All dolls use the Short or Medium Sleeve pattern with Cuff Cutting Line.

Shirley: Sleeve bias bindings are 1" X 4". The skirt tiers are: 1-1/2" X 18"; 2" X 28"; and 2-1/2" X 50".

Violet: Sleeve bias bindings are 1" X 4-1/4". The skirt tiers are: 1-1/2" X 18"; 2" X 28"; and 2-1/2" X 50".

Götz/Pleasant Co.: Sleeve bias bindings are 1" X 5". The skirt tiers are the same as for Angel.

Hilary/T.J. 501: Sleeve bias bindings are 1" X 4-1/4". The skirt tiers are the same as for Angel.

Christina/T.J. 512: Sleeve bias bindings are 1" X 4-1/4". The skirt tiers are: 1-3/4" X 20"; 2-1/4" X 32"; and 3-1/4" X 55".

Jenny/Emily: Sleeve bias bindings are 1" X 4-1/4". The skirt tiers are: 1-3/4" X 25"; 2-1/4" X 37"; 3-1/2" X 60".

May/Seeley MB140S 14": Follow Angel's instructions exactly.

Elise/Georgia: Sleeve bias bindings are 1" X 4-1/2". The skirt tiers are: 2" X 20"; 2-1/2" X 32"; and 3-1/2" X 55".

Shay: Sleeve bias bindings are 1" X 5-1/4". The skirt tiers are: 1-3/4" X 25"; 2-1/4" X 37"; and 3-3/4" X 60".

Tiffany: Sleeve bias bindings are 1" X 5". The skirt tiers are 2" X 25"; 2-3/4" X 37"; and 4" X 60".

Willow: Sleeve bias bindings are 1" X 4-1/2". The skirt tiers are 2-1/2" X 25"; 3-1/4" X 37"; and 4-1/2" X 60".

Heidi: Sleeve bias bindings are 1" X 5-3/4". The skirt tiers are 1-3/4" X 30"; 2-1/4" X 42"; and 3-3/4" X 65".

In the good old days, photographers made house calls. Jean (no sense of humor yet) and Joyce, 1953

Tiffany's Plaid Dress

(Tiffany's body is from the pattern provided by the mold company.)

Supplies:

2/3 yd. Madras plaid fabric
Scrap of white broadcloth for collar and cuffs
6-10" tiny white piping
5 to 7 buttons for front embellishment, 3/8" size**
     (for Tiffany, Shay, Willow, Heidi; smaller dolls use 1/4")
1 yd. grosgrain ribbon for belt, 5/8" wide
3 small snaps

BODICE

Cut out two fronts and four backs from plaid fabric, using Waist Dress bodice pieces.

Cut out four Small Peter Pan Collar pieces from the white broadcloth as indicated on the pattern and assemble according to Basic Instructions for Peter Pan Collars.

Pin piping to right side of front bodice, according to the curved guideline on the Waist Dress Bodice pattern piece. Make sure the piping is towards the collar and the unfinished fabric edge of the piping is towards the lower edge of the bodice. Stitch over the original piping stitching line. Trim away most of the excess fabric from the piping and flip the piping over towards the lower

Karen Cermak in 1959

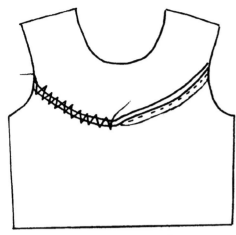

Sewing Piping to Bodice

A Classic Betsy McCall '50s Dress

Karen Cermak (right)
and Sister Roberta

edge of the bodice, hiding the piping seam allowance. Blind hem stitch or zig-zag the piping in place this way.

Place collar on the right side of the bodice as shown and baste to bodice neckline.

Right sides together, sew lining to bodice, sandwiching collar between them, stitching up the center backs and around the neckline, just as you would normally sew the bodice together even if there were no collar there. Do not sew side seams yet.

Cut out two sleeves from dress fabric, using Medium Sleeve pattern piece with Cuff Cutting Line.

Cut out two 2" X 5" cuff pieces on grain from white broadcloth.

Assemble sleeves according to Basic Instructions for Gathered Sleeve with Cuff. Attach sleeves to bodice and then sew underarm sleeves according to Basic Instructions.

Arrange the 5 to 7 buttons so that they are pleasantly and evenly spaced across the front of the bodice, above the piping. Sew in place.

SKIRT

Cut a rectangle 8-1/2" X 45". Sew center back seam and hem skirt bottom as directed in Basic Instructions.

Gather and attach the skirt according to Basic Instructions #10. Lapping right back over left back, sew three snaps to dress bodice.

Tie the ribbon around the waist for a belt with a bow in back.

WHAT TO DO FOR OTHER DOLLS

All dolls use the Short or Medium Sleeve pattern with Cuff Cutting Line.

Shirley: Sleeve cuffs are 1-1/2" X 4". The skirt is 5-1/2" X 30".
Violet: Sleeve cuffs are 1-1/2" X 4-1/4". The skirt is 5-1/4" X 38".
Götz/Pleasant Co.: Use Short Sleeve pattern with Cuff Cutting Line. Sleeve cuffs are 2" X 5". The skirt is 6-1/4" X 45".
Hilary/T.J. 501: Sleeve cuffs are 2" X 4". The skirt is 6-1/2" X 45".
Christina/T.J. 512: Sleeve cuffs are 2" X 4". The skirt is 7" X 45".
Jenny/Emily: Sleeve cuffs are 2" X 4-1/4". The skirt is 7-1/4" X 45".
Angel/May/Seeley ALB9873/MB140S 14": Sleeve cuffs are 2" X 4-1/4". The skirt is 6-1/2" X 45".
Elise/Georgia: Sleeve cuffs are 2" X 4-1/2". The skirt is 7-3/4" X 45".
Shay: Sleeve cuffs are 2" X 5-1/4". The skirt is 7-1/2" X 45".
Willow: Sleeve cuffs are 2" X 4-1/2". The skirt is 10" X 45".
Heidi: Sleeve cuffs are 2" X 5-3/4". The skirt is 7-1/2" X 45".

Jenny's Turquoise Waist Dress and Pinafore (Front Cover)

(Jenny's body is from the pattern provided by the mold company.)

<u>Supplies:</u>

2/3 yd. taffeta
2/3 yd. nylon organdy for collar and pinafore
5 small snaps

DRESS BODICE

Cut out two fronts and four backs from taffeta, using Waist Dress bodice pieces. Assemble bodice and bodice lining according to Basic Instructions, but do not sew lining to bodice yet.

Cut out four Small Peter Pan Collar pieces from the white organdy as indicated on the pattern and assemble according to Basic Instructions for Peter Pan Collars.

Place collar on the right side of the bodice as shown and baste to bodice neckline.

Right sides together, sew lining to bodice, sandwiching collar between them, stitching up the center backs and around the neckline, just as you would normally sew the bodice together even if there were no collar there. Do not sew side seams yet.

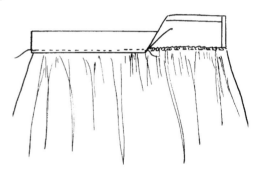

Waistband to Pinafore Skirt

Cut out two sleeves using Short Sleeve pattern piece with Cuff Cutting Line and two bias strips 1" X 4-1/4" for sleeve binding.

Assemble sleeves according to Basic Instructions for Puffed Sleeve with Narrow Binding. Attach sleeves to bodice and then sew underarm sleeves according to Basic Instructions.

DRESS SKIRT

Cut a rectangle 7-1/4" X 45". Sew center back seam and hem skirt bottom as directed in Basic Instructions.

Gather and attach the skirt according to Basic Instructions #10. Lapping right back over left back, sew three snaps to dress bodice.

PINAFORE

From nylon organdy cut out the pinafore skirt 7-1/4" X 45"; the waistband 2" X 12-1/2"; two fronts and four backs from Pinafore Bib pattern pieces; two ruffles 3" X 20"; and two ties 2" X 18" each.

Cutting Ruffle Shape

Gather top of pinafore skirt to fit waistband. Pin the wrong side of the skirt to the right side of the waistband, with the waistband extending 1/4" beyond the

50

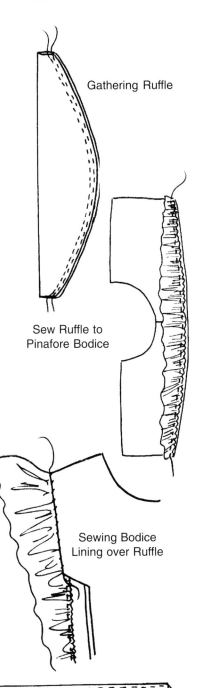

Gathering Ruffle

Sew Ruffle to
Pinafore Bodice

Sewing Bodice
Lining over Ruffle

Pinafore Tie

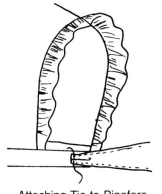

Attaching Tie to Pinafore

skirt. Stitch in place. Press the remaining long edge of the waistband 1/4" toward the wrong side. Tucking in the short ends of the waistband, fold the waistband over to the right side and topstitch all three sides. Set aside.

Sew shoulder seams of pinafore yoke and pinafore yoke lining as you would in the beginning of Basic Instructions for bodices/yokes. Right sides together, sew pinafore yoke to yoke lining, stitching center backs and around neckline. Trim seam allowances, turn right side out and press.

Now, if you've ever sewn an angel sleeve onto a child's pinafore, you probably had a long crescent-shaped pattern piece. Because such a pattern piece would not fit in this book, even for a doll-sized garment, you will make a crescent-shaped ruffle from the rectangular pieces you cut earlier.

First, take a look back at Hannah's Teapot Pinafore, page 45. Because that angel sleeve did not go over the shoulder, front to back, it was shorter and could be an actual pattern piece. For Jenny's pinafore, you must first take the rectangle you cut for the ruffle and fold it in half lengthwise, right sides together; press. Then fold it in half cross-wise, so that the front and back of each ruffle can be cut simultaneously, so they match. Cut the long raw edge (as opposed to the folded edge) of each ruffle so that it is shaped like Hannah's ruffle. This is not an exact process, just an eyeball operation.

Now gather the folded ruffle along the curved edge. Pull the gathering threads so that the ruffle fits along the entire side of the pinafore bodice, waistband to waistband. Right sides together, stitch in place.

Press the remaining armhole edge of the pinafore bodice lining 1/4" toward the wrong side, enclosing the raw edges. Slip stitch to ruffle.

PINAFORE TIES

Narrow hem both long edges of each tie. On one end of each tie, fold the fabric, right sides together, at a 45 degree angle so that the end meets the long edge. Stitch. Turn to right side and press.

Make a small pleat in the remaining short end of the tie so that it fits on the pinafore waistband. Fold 1/4" toward the wrong side and stitch to the waistband where the side seam would be.

Pin bib front to center front of pinafore skirt, with unfinished edge of bib slightly below the waistband seam. Stitch over the waistband seam to secure bib. Similarly, sew the pinafore bodice backs to the pinafore skirt backs, lining up center backs.

Lapping right over left 1/4", sew one snap to the waistband and one snap to the top of the pinafore's center back.

WHAT TO DO FOR OTHER DOLLS

All dolls can use the Short or Medium Sleeve pattern piece for their size, with Cuff Cutting Line.

Shirley: The dress skirt is: 5-1/2" X 30"; sleeve bias bindings are 1" X 4".

The pinafore skirt is: 4-1/2" X 30"; ties: 1-1/2" X 14" each; ruffles are 3" X 16" each.

Violet: The dress skirt is 5-1/4" X 38"; sleeve bias bindings are 1" X 4-1/4". The pinafore skirt is: 4-1/4" X 38"; ties: 1-1/2" X 14" each; ruffles are 3" X 16" each.

Götz/Pleasant Co.: The dress skirt is: 6-1/4" X 45"; sleeve bias bindings are 1" X 5". The pinafore skirt is: 5-1/4" X 45"; ties are 2" X 18" each; ruffles are 3" X 20" each.

Hilary/T.J. 501: The dress skirt is: 6-1/2" X 45"; sleeve bias bindings are 1" X 4". The pinafore skirt is: 5-1/2" X 45"; ties are 2" X 18" each; ruffles are 3" X 20" each.

Christina/T.J. 512: The dress skirt is: 7" X 45"; sleeve bias bindings are 1" X 4". The pinafore skirt is: 6" X 45"; ties are 2" X 18" each; ruffles are 3" X 18" each.

Emily: Follow Jenny's instructions exactly.

Angel/May/Seeley ALB9873/MB140S 14": The dress skirt is 6-1/2" X 45"; sleeve bias bindings are 1" X 4-1/4". The pinafore skirt is: 5-1/2" X 45"; ties are 2" X 18" each; ruffles are 3" X 20" each.

Elise/Georgia: The dress skirt is 7-3/4" X 45"; sleeve bias bindings are 1" X 4-1/2". The pinafore skirt is: 6-3/4" X 45"; ties are 2" X 18" each; ruffles are 4" X 20" each.

Shay: The dress skirt is 7-1/2" X 45"; sleeve bias bindings are 1" X 5-1/4". The pinafore skirt is: 6-1/2" X 45"; ties are 2" X 18" each; ruffles are 3" X 20" each.

Tiffany: The dress skirt is 8-1/2" X 45" sleeve bias bindings are 1" X 5". The pinafore skirt is: 7-1/2" X 45; ties are 2" X 18" each; ruffles are 3" X 24" each.

Willow: The dress requires 2/3 yd. fabric, and its skirt is 10" X 45"; sleeve bias bindings are 1" X 4-1/2". The pinafore skirt is: 9" X 45"; ties are 2" X 18" each; ruffles are 4" X 30" each.

Heidi: The dress skirt is 7-1/2" X 45"; sleeve bias bindings are 1" X 5-3/4". The pinafore skirt is 6-1/2" X 45"; ties are 2" X 21" each; ruffles are 4" X 30" each.

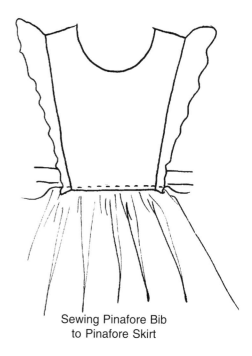

Sewing Pinafore Bib
to Pinafore Skirt

Anne's Pink and Black Christmas Dress (Back Cover)

(Anne is an 18" vinyl Götz doll with non-articulated shoulder and hip joints. Compare Anne's body to the one next to her, redheaded Ginger. Ginger's body is identical to the Pleasant Company's American Girl dolls, also manufactured by Götz Dolls. Articulated joints or not, these dolls share the same measurements and pattern pieces.)

Supplies:

2/3 yd. pink nylon organdy
1/3 yd. pink taffeta for underskirt
1/4 yd. black velveteen
1/4 yd. black lining fabric
28" flat lace, 3/8" wide
90" black soutache braid

Karen and Roberta
with all the right accessories

3 snaps
2 decorative buttons, approximately 1/4" to 3/8"
1 ribbon rose/fake silk flower with leaves

BODICE

Cut out one front and two backs from the black velveteen, using Waist Dress pattern pieces. Cut out one front and two backs from the black lining fabric, using the same pattern pieces.

Assemble bodice and bodice lining according to Basic Instructions.

From the pink nylon organdy, cut out two sleeves, using Short Sleeve pattern piece with Cuff Cutting Line, and two bias strips 1" X 5" for sleeve binding.

Assemble sleeves according to Basic Instructions for Puffed Sleeve with Narrow Binding. Attach sleeves to bodice and then sew underarm sleeves according to Basic Instructions.

BODICE TRIM

Because with doll clothes you are working with tiny seam allowances, and things can shift around a bit on you as you sew, we recommend trimming the bodice after it is sewn together. This way, the "V" of the lace ends up exactly where it's supposed to, instead of off center.

Place the flat lace on the bodice front along the "V" marked on the pattern piece. Be sure to turn under the short ends of the lace 1/4" at the shoulder seam and miter the lace at the center of the "V". Whip stitch the lace to the velveteen bodice.

Applying Lace Trim

Gather the remaining lace, turning under the short ends of it 1/4", and whip stitch it to the neckline as shown.

Sew two decorative buttons to the center front as shown.

SKIRT

Cut a rectangle of the nylon organdy and also a rectangle of the taffeta underlining 6-1/4" X 45". On both pieces, hem one long side of the fabric by pressing it under 1/4", then pressing it under another 1". Stitch hem in place on both pieces.

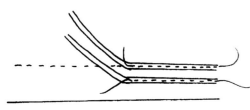

Soutache Braid Goes
Over Stitching

Top stitch into place on the nylon organdy a line of soutache braid on top of the hem stitching. Top stitch into place a second line of soutache braid 1/4" below the first line (3/4" from the hemmed skirt bottom).

Treating the organdy skirt and taffeta underlining as one unit, sew center back seam and placket according to Basic Instructions. Again treating both layers as one unit, gather the top edge of the skirt to fit the bodice. Right sides together, sew the skirt to the bodice. Lapping right back over left back, sew 3 evenly spaced snaps to the bodice center back.

Tack a ribbon rose or fake silk flower to the waist of the dress, off center.

WHAT TO DO FOR OTHER DOLLS

All dolls can use the Short or Medium Sleeve pattern piece for their size, with Cuff Cutting Line.

Shirley: The dress skirt is: 5-1/2" X 30"; sleeve bias bindings are 1" X 4". Lace: 19"; soutache braid: 60".
Violet: The dress skirt is 5-1/4" X 38"; sleeve bias bindings are 1" X 4-1/4". Lace: 25"; soutache braid: 76".
Hilary/T.J. 501: The dress skirt is: 6-1/2" X 45"; sleeve bias bindings are 1" X 4". Lace: 25"; soutache braid: 90".
Christina/T.J. 512: The dress skirt is: 7" X 45"; sleeve bias bindings are 1" X 4". Lace: 25"; soutache braid: 90".
Emily/Jenny: The dress skirt is 7-1/4" X 45"; sleeve bias bindings are 1" X 4-1/4". Lace: 28"; soutache braid: 90".
Angel/May/Seeley ALB9873/MB140S 14": The dress skirt is 6-1/2" X 45"; sleeve bias bindings are 1" X 4-1/4". Lace: 25"; soutache braid: 90".
Elise/Georgia: The dress skirt is 7-3/4" X 45"; sleeve bias bindings are 1" X 4-1/2". Lace: 25"; soutache braid: 90".
Shay: The dress skirt is 7-1/2" X 45"; sleeve bias bindings are 1" X 5-1/4". Lace: 28"; soutache braid: 90".
Tiffany: The dress skirt is 8-1/2" X 45" sleeve bias bindings are 1" X 5". Lace: 25"; soutache braid: 90".
Willow: The dress skirt is 10" X 45"; sleeve bias bindings are 1" X 4-1/2". Lace: 25"; soutache braid: 90".
Heidi: The dress skirt is 7-1/2" X 45"; sleeve bias bindings are 1" X 5-3/4". Lace: 28"; soutache braid: 90".

Joan's Kindergarten Graduation Dress--Poofy!

Willow's Apple Plaid Shirtwaist Dress

(Willow's body is from the pattern provided by the mold company.)

Supplies:

2/3 yd. plaid fabric
Scrap of white broadcloth for collar and cuffs
1 package baby size Rick-Rack
12" red satin ribbon, 1/4" wide
5 apple buttons, approximately 1/2"
6 small snaps

This dress opens down the entire front, like a robe. Be sure you cut out the right bodice pieces.

BODICE

Cut out four fronts and two backs from plaid fabric, using Shirtwaist Dress bodice pieces and Dress Cutting Line.

Cut out two Large Pointed Collar pieces from the white broadcloth as indi-

It's amazing we didn't
all succumb to Rick Rack poisoning

cated on the pattern. Right sides together, sew collar to collar lining by stitching around the outside curved edge and up the center fronts. Do not sew around neckline. Trim away excess seam allowance, turn right side out and press. Top stitch Rick-Rack around the finished edges of the collar, mitering the front corners.

Place collar on the right side of the bodice as shown and baste to bodice neckline.

Right sides together, sew lining to bodice, sandwiching collar between them, stitching up the center fronts and around the neckline, just as you would normally sew the bodice together even if there were no collar there. Do not sew side seams yet.

Cut out two sleeves from dress fabric, using Medium Sleeve pattern piece with Cuff Cutting Line.

Cut out two 2" X 4-1/2" cuff pieces on grain from white broadcloth.

Assemble sleeves according to Basic Instructions for Gathered Sleeve with Cuff. Before attaching sleeves to bodice, top stitch Rick-Rack around the top of each cuff so that it covers and seam between sleeve and cuff.

Attach sleeves to bodice and then sew underarm sleeves according to Basic Instructions.

SKIRT

Cut a rectangle 10" X 45". Hem the center fronts (the two short ends of the rectangle) by pressing them under 1/4" twice, then stitching. Hem the lower edge of the skirt by pressing it up 1/4", then another 1" and stitching.

Top stitch one row of Rick-Rack over the hem line and another row of it 1/2" above the first row, tucking under the ends of the Rick-Rack 1/4".

Gather and attach the skirt according to Basic Instructions, #10.

Lapping Right front over left front, sew three snaps to bodice front, spacing them evenly between neck edge and waist/skirt seam. Sew three more snaps between waist and top row of Rick-Rack, spacing them evenly.

Joan in Plaid

Sew decorative apple buttons over each snap except the one at the neck. Make a bow of the red ribbon and tack it over the neckline snap.

WHAT TO DO FOR OTHER DOLLS

All dolls use the Short or Medium Sleeve pattern with Cuff Cutting Line.

Shirley: Sleeve cuffs are 1-1/2" X 4". The skirt is 5-1/2" X 30".
Violet: Sleeve cuffs are 1-1/2" X 4-1/4". The skirt is 5-1/4" X 38".
Götz/Pleasant Co.: Sleeve cuffs are 2" X 5". The skirt is 6-1/4" X 45".
Hilary/T.J. 501: Sleeve cuffs are 2" X 4". The skirt is 6-1/2" X 45".
Christina/T.J. 512: Sleeve cuffs are 2" X 4". The skirt is 7" X 45".
Jenny/Emily: Sleeve cuffs are 2" X 4-1/4". The skirt is 7-1/4" X 45".

Angel/May/Seeley ALB9873/MB140S 14": Sleeve cuffs are 2" X 4-1/4". The skirt is 6-1/2" X 45".
Elise/Georgia: Sleeve cuffs are 2" X 4-1/2". The skirt is 7-3/4" X 45".
Shay: Sleeve cuffs are 2" X 5-1/4". The skirt is 7-1/2" X 45".
Tiffany: Sleeve cuffs are 2" X 5". The skirt is 8-1/2"X 45".
Heidi: Sleeve cuffs are 2" X 5-3/4". The skirt is 7-1/2" X 45".

Emily's Plaid Suspender Skirt and Blouse

(Emily's body is from the pattern provided by the mold company.)

Supplies:

1/4 yd. white broadcloth for blouse
4 buttons, 1/8"
4 small snaps
12" red satin ribbon for bow, 1/4" wide
1/2 yd. plaid flannel or wool fabric for skirt
3 medium snaps
3 buttons, 3/8" (optional)

BLOUSE

This blouse opens down the front.

Cut out four fronts and two backs from white broadcloth, using Shirtwaist Dress bodice pieces and Blouse Cutting Line.

Cut out two Medium One Piece Peter Pan Collar pieces from the white broadcloth as indicated on the pattern. Right sides together, sew collar to collar lining by stitching around the outside curved edge. Do not sew around neckline. Trim away excess seam allowance, turn right side out and press.

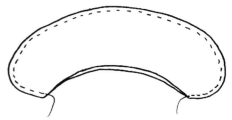

One-Piece Peter Pan Collar

Place collar on the right side of the bodice as shown and baste to bodice neckline.

Right sides together, sew lining to bodice, sandwiching collar between them, stitching up the center fronts and around the neckline, just as you would normally sew the bodice together even if there were no collar there. Do not sew side seams yet.

Cut out two sleeves from white broadcloth, using Medium Sleeve pattern piece with Cuff Cutting Line.

Cut out two bias strips 1" X 4-1/4" from white broadcloth.

Assemble sleeves according to Basic Instructions for Puffed Sleeve with Narrow Binding.

Attach sleeves to bodice and then sew underarm sleeves according to Basic

Joyce in suspender skirt, 1948. Joan and her sisters wore identical ensembles in the '50s.

56

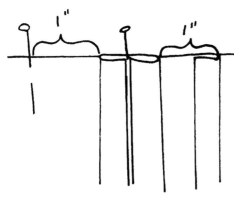

Center Front Pleat

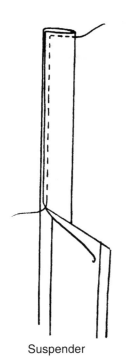

Suspender

Attaching Suspenders to Skirt

Instructions.

Zig-zag or serge lower edge of blouse to finish. Lapping right front over left front, sew four snaps to the center front opening, spacing them evenly. If you wish, sew four small decorative buttons on top of snaps. Tie the ribbon in a bow and tack it over the top button.

SKIRT

Cut a rectangle of plaid fabric 7-1/2" X 26". Cut a waistband 2" X 13-1/4" and two suspenders 1-1/4" X 11-1/2" each.

Hem skirt bottom as directed in Basic Instructions, but do not sew center back seam yet.

On the wrong side of the skirt, mark the center front of it with a pin (middle of one long edge of the rectangle). Place a pin on both sides of the center front 1/2" from the center. Make a pleat (still on the wrong side of the fabric) by bringing the two side pins to meet the center one. Baste in place. You now have one reversed box pleat.

With the skirt rectangle now right side up, place pins at 1" intervals, starting at the two folds at the center front. At each pin, make a 1/2" knife pleat going away from the center. Baste across the top of the skirt to hold the pleats in place, then press the knife pleats from waist to bottom edge of skirt.

Pin the wrong side of the skirt to the right side of the waistband, with the waistband extending 1/4" beyond the skirt. Because all the dolls' waists vary and your pleats may vary somewhat in precision, be prepared to do a little easing or stretching of the skirt pleats in back to match the waistband. If the back pleats come too close to the center back opening, make them slightly closer together to even things out. Stitch in place. Press the remaining long edge of the waistband 1/4" toward the wrong side. Tucking in the short ends of the waistband, fold the waistband over to the right side and topstitch all three sides.

To finish off the suspenders, press under each long edge 1/4". Fold each suspender in half lengthwise, right sides out, tucking in the short ends 1/4". Top stitch along the three edges to be finished.

Try the skirt on the doll and pin suspenders to inside of garment front at waistband, each suspender an equal distance from the center front pleat so that they go relatively straight up the chest and over the shoulder. Stitch over the waistband seam to secure suspenders.

Lapping right over left 1/4", sew a snap to the waistband.

Sew one-half of a snap to the back waistband 1" to the left and right of the center back. Try the skirt on the doll, crossing the suspenders in back, and mark the suspenders where the other half of the snaps should be. Sew them in place.

WHAT TO DO FOR OTHER DOLLS

All dolls use the Short or Medium Sleeve pattern with Cuff Cutting Line.

Shirley: Sleeve bias bindings are 1" X 4". The skirt is 6" X 19"; the waist-band: 1-1/2" X 10"; and the suspenders are: 1-1/4" X 9" each.
Violet: Sleeve bias bindings are 1" X 4-1/4". The skirt is 5-3/4" X 22"; the waistband: 1-1/2" X 11"; and the suspenders are: 1-1/4" X 9" each.
Götz/Pleasant Co.: Sleeve bias bindings are 1" X 5". The skirt is 6-1/4" X 24"; the waistband: 2" X 12"; and the suspenders are: 1-1/4" X 11" each.
Hilary/T.J. 501/Christina/T.J. 512: Sleeve bias bindings are 1" X 4". The skirt is 7" X 22"; the waistband: 2" X 11"; and the suspenders are: 1-1/4" X 11" each.
Jenny: Follow Emily's instructions exactly.
Angel/May/Seeley ALB9873/MB140S 14": Sleeve bias bindings are 1" X 4-1/4". The skirt is 7" X 22"; the waistband: 2" X 11"; and the suspenders are 1-1/4" X 11" each.
Elise/Georgia: Sleeve bias bindings are 1" X 4-1/2". The skirt is 8-1/4" X 24"; the waistband 2" X 12"; and the suspenders are: 1-1/4" X 11-1/2" each.
Shay: Sleeve bias bindings are 1" X 5-1/4". The skirt is 7-1/2" X 23"; the waistband: 2" X 11-1/4"; and the suspenders are: 1-1/4" X 11" each.
Tiffany: Sleeve bias bindings are 1" X 5". The skirt is 8-1/4" X 22"; the waistband: 2" X 11"; and the suspenders are: 1-1/4" X 12" each.
Willow: Sleeve bias bindings are 1" X 5-3/4". The skirt is 10" X 28"; the waistband 2" X 13-3/4"; and the suspenders are: 1-1/4" X 15".
Heidi: Sleeve bias bindings are 2" X 5-3/4". The skirt is 7-1/4" X 30"; the waistband: 2" X 14-3/4"; and the suspenders are: 1-1/4" X 13" each.

Jenny, Joan and Ellen, 1962

Shay's Gingham Smocked Yoke Dress

(Shay's body is from the pattern provided by the mold company.)

Supplies:

2/3 yd. gingham fabric
Scrap of white broadcloth for collar and cuffs
1/4 yd. tiny piping
Pink and white embroidery floss
3 small snaps

BODICE

Cut out two fronts and four backs using Yoke Dress bodice pieces. Assemble bodice and bodice lining according to Basic Instructions, but do not sew lining to bodice yet.

Cut out four Small Peter Pan Collar pieces from the white broadcloth as indicated on the pattern and assemble according to Basic Instructions for Peter Pan Collars.

Place collar on the right side of the bodice as shown and baste to bodice neckline.

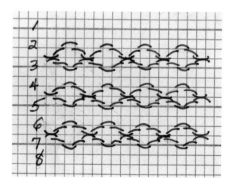

58

Right sides together, sew lining to bodice, sandwiching collar between them, stitching up the center backs and around the neckline, just as you would normally sew the bodice together even if there were no collar there.

Cut out two sleeves from gingham, using Medium Sleeve pattern piece with Cuff Cutting Line. Cut out two cuffs on grain from white broadcloth 2" X 5-1/4".

Assemble sleeves according to Basic Instructions for Gathered Sleeve with Cuff. Attach sleeves to bodice and then sew underarm sleeves according to Basic Instructions.

SMOCKED SKIRT

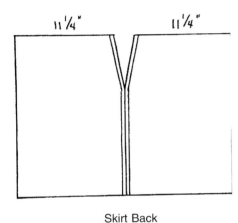

Skirt Back

Cut a rectangle of gingham 9-3/4" X 45". Fold it in half cross-wise so you have a rectangle 9-3/4" X 22-1/2". Cut the fabric in half along the fold line. Now you have a front and a back skirt.

Fold the back skirt in half so that you have a rectangle 9-3/4" X 11-1/4". Cut the fabric in half along the fold line. Now you have a left back and a right back skirt. Sew center back seam and finish placket as directed in Basic Instructions, #8, but do not hem. Gather the tops of the skirt backs and set aside.

Starting 1/4" in from top edge of skirt front, pleat it with 8 half-space rows. Pull the gathering threads so that the skirt front is 6-3/4" wide. Smock according to smocking graph, beginning on row 2 of the pleating. When smocking is completed, remove all pleating threads except the top one.

Pin piping to top of skirt front, right sides together, so that the stitching line of the piping runs along the top pleating thread. Stitch, following the top pleating thread.

Right sides together, sew smocked skirt front to skirt backs at side seams. To hem, turn up bottom of skirt 1/4" and press. Turn up another 1" and stitch.

Piping on Skirt Front

Pull gathering threads of skirt backs so that when you pin the bodice to the skirt, right sides together, they match. Stitch. Lapping right back over left back, sew three snaps to dress bodice.

Embroider pink lazy daisies to collar fronts as indicated on pattern piece.

WHAT TO DO FOR OTHER DOLLS

**For all other dolls, pull the pleating threads of the front skirt to match bottom edge of the individual doll's front yoke pattern piece.

All dolls use the Short or Medium Sleeve pattern with Cuff Cutting Line.

Shirley: Sleeve cuffs are 1-1/2" X 4". The skirt is 6" X 38".
Violet: Sleeve cuffs are 1-1/2" X 4-1/4". The skirt is 5-3/4" X 40".
Götz/Pleasant Co.: Sleeve cuffs are 2" X 5". The skirt is 7-1/4" X 45".
Hilary/T.J. 501: Sleeve cuffs are 2" X 4". The skirt is 7" X 45".
Christina/T.J. 512: Sleeve cuffs are 2" X 4". The skirt is 7-3/4" X 45".

Jenny/Emily: Use Medium Sleeve pattern with Cuff Cutting Line. Sleeve cuffs are 2" X 4-1/4". The skirt is 8-3/4" X 45".
Angel/May/Seeley ALB9873/MB140S 14": Sleeve cuffs are 2" X 4-1/4". The skirt is 7-3/4" X 45".
Elise/Georgia: Sleeve cuffs are 2" X 4-1/2". The skirt is 8-3/4" X 45".
Tiffany: Sleeve cuffs are 2" X 5". The skirt is 9" X 45".
Willow: Sleeve cuffs are 2" X 4-1/2". The skirt is 11-1/2" X 45".
Heidi: Sleeve cuffs are 2" X 5-3/4". The skirt is 9" X 45".

May's Carnaby Street Mini-Dress

(May's body is Seeley's composition MB140S 14")

<u>Supplies:</u>

1/2 yd. "op art" print fabric (geometrics, neons)
1-1/4" long scrap of 3/8" ribbon
2 small snaps

BODICE

Cut out two fronts and four backs, using Square-Necked Yoke Dress pattern pieces. Right sides together, sew each front to two backs at the shoulder seams, so that you have a bodice and a bodice lining.

Right sides together, sew the bodice to its lining by stitching along the center back edges and around the square neckline. Then stitch bodice and lining together around armholes. Clip curves and trim seam allowances. Turn right side out by pulling the backs through the shoulder seams. Press.

Stitch the side seams together by opening up the bodice and lining at the armholes. Press and set aside.

SKIRT

Cut out a rectangle 7-1/4" X 21". Mark the center of the long side of the rectangle with a pin (on May, that's at the 10-1/2" point). Place pins 1-1/2" to both sides of the first pin. Working from the right side of the fabric, create a box pleat by drawing the two outside pins to the center pin. Baste in place and press.

Sew center back seam and hem skirt bottom as directed in Basic Instructions.

Gather and attach the skirt according to Basic Instructions #10. Lapping right back over left back, sew two snaps to dress bodice.

DECORATIVE BOW

Cut a rectangle of fabric 2" X 6". Narrow hem the long sides. Fold under the ends of the rectangle so that it resembles a 2-3/4" wide bow. Pinch the fabric together in the middle and wrap it with the scrap of ribbon. Hand stitch the

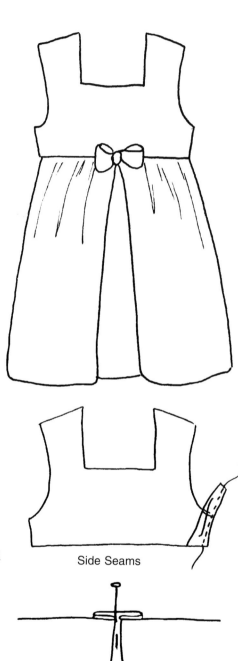

Side Seams

Center Pleat

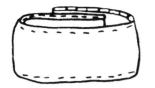

Narrow Hem and Fold Fabric

Finished Bow

ribbon and fabric together, then tack it in place at the center front of the dress, right above the pleat.

WHAT TO DO FOR OTHER DOLLS

Shirley: Skirt is 6" X 24". Bow is 1-1/2" X 4-1/2", because this doll body is so very slim.
Violet: The skirt is 5-3/4" X 28".
Götz/Pleasant Co.: The skirt is 7-1/4" X 30".
Hilary/T.J. 501: The skirt is 7" X 30".
Jenny/Emily: The skirt is 8-3/4" X 30".
Angel/Seeley ALB9873: Follow instructions for May exactly.
Christina/T.J. 512: The skirt is 7-3/4" X 30".
Elise/Georgia: The skirt is 8-3/4" X 30".
Shay: The skirt is 8-3/4" X 36".
Tiffany: The skirt is 9" X 36".
Willow: The skirt is 11-1/2" X 36" and you make the center pleat by measuring 2" in each direction from the center.
Heidi: The skirt is 9" X 40" and you make the center pleat by measuring 2" in each direction from the center.

Hilary's Baby Doll Mini and Vest

(Hilary's body is the porcelain T.J. 501)

<u>Supplies:</u>

2/3 yd. loud and obnoxious print fabric
2 small snaps

BODICE

Cut out two fronts and four backs using Scoop-Necked Yoke Dress bodice pieces. Assemble bodice according to Basic Instructions.

Cut out two sleeves using Short Sleeve pattern piece with Cuff Cutting Line and two bias strips 1" X 4" for sleeve binding.

Assemble sleeves according to Basic Instructions for Puffed Sleeve with Narrow Binding. Attach sleeves to bodice and then sew underarm sleeves according to Basic Instructions.

SKIRT

Cut a rectangle 6-1/2" X 30". Sew center back seam and hem skirt bottom as directed in Basic Instructions.

Make one box pleat in center front of skirt by doing the following: Mark the center front of the skirt on the unhemmed edge. Measure 1-1/2" on both sides of the center and mark those places with pins. With the right side of the skirt facing you, bring the pins to the center mark and baste the pleat in place.

See center pleat diagram on page 60.

Gather and attach the skirt according to Basic Instructions, #10.

Lapping right back over left back, sew two snaps to dress bodice.

MOCK CROCHETED VEST

Supplies:

1/3 yd. open weave cotton fabric (curtain fabric?)

Cut out two fronts and one back, using Vest pattern pieces. Using zig-zag stitch or serger, sew fronts to back at shoulder and side seams. This type of garment was intended to look raggedy, so no hemming or finishing of edges is done. Similar to net-based lace, most open weave fabrics will not ravel.

WHAT TO DO FOR OTHER DOLLS
Follow sleeve instructions for Jenny's Turquoise (cover) dress.
Shirley: Skirt is 6" X 24".
Violet: The skirt is 5-3/4" X 28".
Götz/Pleasant Co.: The skirt is 7-1/4" X 30".
Jenny/Emily: The skirt is 8-3/4" X 30".
Angel/May/Seeley ALB9873/MB140S 14": The skirt is 7-3/4" X 30"
Christina/T.J. 20": The skirt is 7-1/2" X 30".
Elise/Georgia: The skirt is 8-3/4" X 30".
Shay: The skirt is 8-3/4" X 36".
Tiffany: The skirt is 9" X 36".
Willow: The skirt is 11-1/2" X 36" and you make the center pleat by measuring 2" in each direction from the center.
Heidi: The skirt is 9" X 40" and you make the center pleat by measuring 2" in each direction from the center.

Here's proof that Joan went to a Beatles concert in Minneapolis in 1965. She paid $2.50 for a cheap seat. The good ones were $5.50.

Pui Ling's Denim Daisy Jumper and Blouse

(Pui Ling is an 18" vinyl Götz doll with non-articulated shoulder and hip joints, the same cloth body as that of Anne--last doll in the first page of naked doll photos. Compare Anne's body to the one next to her, redheaded Ginger. Ginger's body is identical to the Pleasant Company's American Girl dolls, also manufactured by Götz Dolls. Articulated joints or not, these dolls share the same measurements and pattern pieces.

Supplies for Blouse:

1/4 yd. white broadcloth
1/3 yd. elastic, 1/8" wide
4 tiny buttons, 1/8"
4 small snaps

Supplies for Jumper:

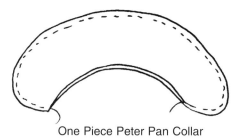

One Piece Peter Pan Collar

1/2 yd. denim
4 daisy appliques (or by-the-yard flower trim)
1 pkg. green baby Rick-Rack
2 small snaps

BLOUSE

This blouse opens down the front.

Cut out four fronts and two backs from white broadcloth, using Shirtwaist Dress bodice pieces and Blouse Cutting Line.

Cut out two Medium One Piece Peter Pan Collar pieces from the white broadcloth as indicated on the pattern. Right sides together, sew collar to collar lining by stitching around the outside curved edge. Do not sew around neckline. Trim away excess seam allowance, turn right side out and press.

Place collar on the right side of the bodice as shown and baste to bodice neckline.

Right sides together, sew lining to bodice, sandwiching collar between them, stitching up the center fronts and around the neckline, just as you would normally sew the bodice together even if there were no collar there. Do not sew side seams yet.

Cut out two sleeves from white broadcloth, using Medium Sleeve pattern piece with Elastic Cutting Line.

Assemble sleeves according to Basic Instructions for Elastic Sleeve Bottom with Ruffle. Elastic required is 8-1/2" cut in half.

Attach sleeves to bodice and then sew underarm sleeves according to Basic Instructions.

Zig-zag or serge lower edge of blouse to finish. Lapping right front over left front, sew four snaps to the center front opening, spacing them evenly. If you wish, sew four small decorative buttons on top of snaps.

JUMPER

From denim, cut out two fronts and four backs using Jumper Yoke bodice pieces.

Right sides together, sew each front to two backs at the shoulder seams, so that you have a bodice and a bodice lining.

Right sides together, sew the bodice to its lining by stitching along the center back edges and around the neckline. Slip curves, trim seam allowances and turn to right side. Press, turning under armhole edges 1/4" and pin bodice to bodice lining around armholes. Top stitch around armholes and neckline, very close to edges. Right sides together, sew side seams.

For the jumper's skirt, cut out a rectangle 7-1/4" X 30". Hem one long edge of

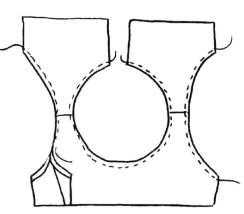

Topstitching Jumper Bodice

the rectangle by pressing the fabric under 1/4", then another 1" and stitching. Machine stitch a line of green Rick Rack over the hem line to represent grass.

Sew center back seam and placket as directed in Basic Instructions.

Gather and attach the skirt according to Basic Instructions #10. Lapping right back over left back, sew two snaps to jumper bodice.

Pin four "stems" of green Rick Rack to perpendicular to "grass," spacing them as you please, varying the heights of the "stems." Pin daisies in place. When you are sure of your design, machine stitch the "stems" in place. The daisies can be glued with fabric glue or hand stitched.

WHAT TO DO FOR OTHER DOLLS

All dolls can use the Short or Medium Sleeve pattern pieces for the blouse, with Elastic Cutting Line.

Shirley: Skirt is 6" X 24". Blouse elastic is 3-1/2" per sleeve.
Violet: The skirt is 5-3/4" X 28". Blouse elastic is 3-1/4" per sleeve.
Hilary/T.J. 501: The skirt is 7-1/4" X 30". Blouse elastic is 3-1/2" per sleeve.
Christina/T.J. 512: The skirt is 7-3/4" X 30". Blouse elastic is 3-1/2" per sleeve.
Jenny/Emily: The skirt is 8-3/4" X 30". Blouse elastic is 3-3/4" per sleeve.
Angel/May/Seeley ALB9873/MB140S 14": The skirt is 6-3/4" X 30". Blouse elastic is 3-3/4" per sleeve.
Elise/Georgia: The skirt is 8-3/4" X 30". Blouse elastic is 3-1/2" per sleeve.
Shay: The skirt is 8-3/4" X 36". Blouse elastic is 4" per sleeve.
Tiffany: The skirt is 9" X 36". Blouse elastic is 4-1/4" per sleeve.
Willow: The skirt is 11-1/2" X 36". Blouse elastic is 3-1/4" per sleeve.
Heidi: The skirt is 9" X 40". Blouse elastic is 5" per sleeve.

"Three hundred mothers and daughters attended the May 1 luncheon sponsored by the Zumbro Lutheran Church Women. The women of Bethel Lutheran prepared and served the food.
Mrs. Harley Carlson served as the general chairman of the event, and was also in charge of decorations and programs. She was assisted by the members of Circles 5, 7, and 13. The theme of the luncheon, 'Design for Living,' was carried out throughout the table and stage decorations. The stage was a garden setting in pink and white. White wrought iron lawn furniture and trellises were accented with pink hydrangeas. Table centerpieces were of pink net flowers in white vases. Other table decorations included cardboard mother and daughter models dressed in pink and white gingham, and nut cups trimmed with pink flowers and net. The programs were designed as patterns of mother and daughter dresses."
From the Zumbro Lutheran Church newsletter, Rochester, MN, May 6, 1965.

Georgia's Sunflower Dress, Detached Collar and Floppy Hat

(Georgia's body is from the pattern provided by the mold company.)

Supplies:

1 yd. sunflower print fabric
Scrap of white broadcloth for collar
1/3 yd. elastic, 1/8"
1 yd. brown piping
2-1/2 yd. yellow grosgrain ribbon, 1" wide
1/4 yd. medium weight interfacing
1-1/4 yd. brown picot edge ribbon, 1/2" wide
5 small snaps

BODICE

Cut out two fronts and four backs from sunflower fabric, using Waist Dress

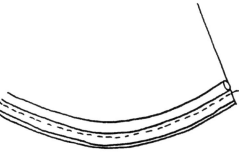

Applying Piping to Collar

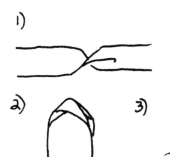

1)

2)   3)

Forming Petals

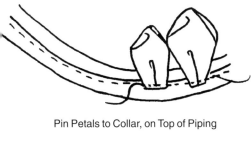

Pin Petals to Collar, on Top of Piping

Hand Stitch Collar Lining Over Petals

bodice pieces. Assemble bodice and bodice lining according to Basic Instructions.

Cut out two sleeves, using Medium Sleeve pattern piece with Elastic Cutting Line.

Assemble sleeves according to Basic Instructions for Elastic Sleeve Bottom with Ruffle. Elastic required is 7" cut in half.

Attach sleeves to bodice and then sew underarm sleeves according to Basic Instructions.

SKIRT

Cut a rectangle 9-1/4" X 45". Sew center back seam and hem skirt bottom as directed in Basic Instructions.

Gather and attach the skirt according to Basic Instructions #10. Lapping right back over left back, sew three snaps to dress bodice.

DETACHED COLLAR

From white broadcloth cut out two fronts and four backs, using Round Collar pattern pieces. Right sides together, sew backs to front of collar at shoulder seams. Repeat for collar lining.

Right sides together, sew the collar lining to the collar, stitching along center back seams and around neckline. Clip curves and trim seam allowances, turn right side out and press.

Sew piping to collar only, not lining.

Cut the yellow grosgrain ribbon into 21 lengths of 3" each. These will be the sunflower petals. Fold each piece of ribbon as shown. Pin the petals to the collar, on top of the piping, arranging them evenly around the perimeter of the collar as shown. Stitch along seam line that attached the piping to the collar. Fold the seam allowances toward the inside so that the petals stick out around the lower edge of the collar.

Press the remaining unfinished edge of the collar lining 1/4" toward the inside. Hand stitch the lining to the petals, closing up and completing the collar. Lapping right over left, sew two snaps to the center back of the collar.

HAT

This hat fits all of the dolls shown in the book, although fullness of wigs can make it fit differently. If you really need to re-size the hat for a completely different size doll, try reducing or enlarging the pattern pieces on a photocopy machine. (Yes, we gladly give you permission to photocopy parts of our book for your own personal use.)

There are three parts to this hat, besides the ribbon embellishment. They are: the crown, which is the top part; the rise, which is the part that connects the crown and the brim; and the brim.

Cut out one crown from the sunflower fabric and one from the interfacing. The rise is a rectangle 1-3/4" X 12-1/2", one cut from sunflower fabric and one cut from interfacing. Cut two brims from the sunflower fabric and one from the interfacing.

Baste interfacing to wrong side of rise, crown and one brim.

Right sides together, sew the remaining brim to the interfaced brim, stitching only around the outside circle. Clip and trim seam allowances, turn right side out and press. Baste all three layers together by stitching around the inner circle. Treat as one layer of fabric from now on.

Make a circle of the interfaced rise by sewing the short ends together (right sides together, of course). Right sides together, sew the rise to the crown. Clip curves and trim seam allowances. Similarly, sew the brim to the rise.

To make sunflower, ruche a 15" length of yellow grosgrain ribbon as shown. Pull the thread tight to form a circle. Pull the front of the hat brim up towards the crown and stitch it that way, applying the yellow "petals" at the same time. Gather 6" of the brown picot ribbon along one long edge. Pull the thread tight to form a circle and tack it to the center of the flower on the hat brim.

Use the remaining brown ribbon to tie around the dress as a belt.

WHAT TO DO FOR OTHER DOLLS

All dolls use the same number of petals on the collar except *Shirley*, who has 20 petals, and *Götz/Pleasant Co.* dolls, who have 23 petals.

Shirley: Skirt is 7" X 30". Sleeve elastic is 3-1/2" per sleeve.
Violet: The skirt is 7-1/2" X 40". Sleeve elastic is 3-1/4" per sleeve.
Götz/Pleasant Co.: The skirt is 8-1/4" X 40". Sleeve elastic is 4-1/4" per sleeve.
Jenny/Emily: The skirt is 8-3/4" X 45". Sleeve elastic is 3-3/4" per sleeve.
Angel/May/Seeley ALB9873/MB140S 14": The skirt is 8-1/2" X 45." Sleeve elastic is 3-3/4" per sleeve.
Hilary/T.J. 501/Christina/T.J. 512: The skirt is 8-1/4" X 45". Sleeve elastic is 3-1/2" per sleeve.
Elise: Follow Georgia's instructions exactly.
Shay: The skirt is 9-1/4" X 45". Sleeve elastic is 4" per sleeve.
Tiffany: The skirt is 9-3/4" X 45". Sleeve elastic is 4-1/4" per sleeve.
Willow: The skirt is 10-3/4" X 45". Sleeve elastic is 3-1/4" per sleeve.
Heidi: The skirt is 9-1/4" X 45". Sleeve elastic is 5" per sleeve.

Heidi's Gardening Jumper and Gingham Blouse

(Heidi's body is from the pattern provided by the mold company.)

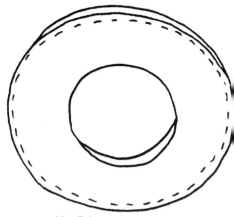

Hat Brim

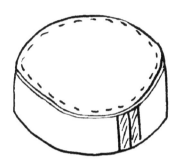

Crown and Rise

Ruching the Yellow Ribbon

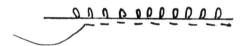

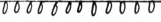

Gather Brown Picot Ribbon

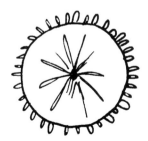

Flower Center

Supplies:

1/4 yd. red gingham for blouse
4 small snaps
1/2 yd. gardening print fabric for jumper
45" gathered eyelet lace, 2" wide for most dolls, 1" wide for Shirley and Violet, 1-1/2" wide for Götz/Pleasant Co.
2 decorative ladybug buttons, approximately 1/2"
4 medium snaps

BLOUSE

This blouse opens down the back.

Cut out two fronts and four backs from the gingham, using the Back Opening Blouse pattern pieces. Assemble bodice and bodice lining according to Basic Instructions, but do not sew lining to bodice yet.

Cut out four Medium Peter Pan Collar pieces from the gingham indicated on the pattern and assemble according to Basic Instructions for Peter Pan Collars.

Right sides together, sew lining to bodice, sandwiching collar between them, stitching up the center backs and around the neckline, just as you would normally sew the bodice together even if there were no collar there.

Cut out two sleeves Short Sleeve pattern piece with Cuff Cutting Line. From the white broadcloth cut two on-grain strips 2" X 5-3/4" for cuff.

Assemble sleeves according to Basic Instructions for Gathered Sleeve with Cuff. Attach sleeves to bodice and then sew underarm sleeves according to Basic Instructions.

Zig-zag or serge lower edge of blouse to finish. Lapping right back over left back, sew four small snaps to the center back opening, spacing them evenly.

JUMPER

From gardening print fabric cut out two jumper straps measuring 1-1/4" X 9". Narrow hem both long edges and one short end of each of the straps.

From gardening print fabric cut out two Gardening Jumper Bibs

Baste the unhemmed ends of the straps to the bib, right sides together, 1-1/4" from short ends of the bib. Sew bib lining to bib, sandwiching the straps in between. Stitch around the center backs and top of the bib as shown, being careful not to catch the straps in the side seams. Trim seam allowances, turn right side out and press.

Cut a rectangle 7-1/4" X 45". Press under one long edge of the rectangle 1/4". Place the heading of the gathered eyelet lace underneath the fold and top stitch in place.

Cut out two pockets 2-1/2" x 2-1/2" each. Press under 1/4" around all four sides of both pockets. Determine the center front of the skirt, then mark points

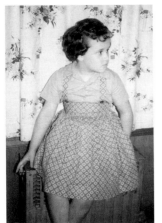

Karen in High-Waisted Skirt/Jumper

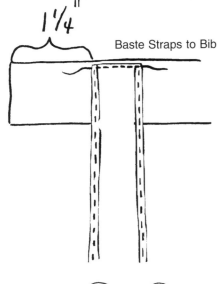

1 1/4"

Baste Straps to Bib

Bib Lining to Bib

67

2" on either side of the center as shown. These points are where the sides of the pockets will be. In other words, there is a 4" gap between the two pockets. Height of the pockets will vary according to the dolls, but a good rule of thumb is that you place them no farther down than 2" from the bib/skirt seam. When you have determined where you want the pockets, top stitch them into place around the three sides and bottom.

Sew center back seam and placket as directed in Basic Instructions.

Gather and attach the skirt according to Basic Instructions #10. Lapping right back over left back, sew two medium snaps to center back of jumper bib.

Put outfit on doll, crossing the straps in back, and mark where you want the snaps for the straps in front. The straps will be of generous length. Sew snaps to jumper bib highest points in front and also to straps. Sew decorative ladybug buttons over the snaps.

The hat is one purchased at a craft shop. We made a bow from gingham, using the pattern for May's Carnaby Street Dress's bow and tacked it in place on the hat.

WHAT TO DO FOR OTHER DOLLS

All dolls use 2" wide eyelet lace 45" long *except the first three listed here*. All dolls except the first three listed also use the same size pockets and placement of them as Heidi does.

All dolls can use the Short or Medium Sleeve pattern piece for their size, with Cuff Cutting Line.

Shirley: Sleeve cuffs are 1-1/2" X 4". The skirt is: 6" X 30"; the eyelet is 1" X 30"; pockets are 2" X 2" and placed 3/4" higher; and the straps are: 1" X 8" each.

Violet: Sleeve cuffs are 1-1/2" X 4-1/4". The skirt is 6-1/2" X 45"; the eyelet is: 1" X 45"; pockets are 2" X 2" and placed 3/4" higher; and the straps are: 1" X 8" each.

Götz/Pleasant Co.: Sleeve cuffs are 2" X 5". The skirt is 6-3/4" X 45"; the eyelet is: 1-1/2" X 45"; pockets are 2" X 2" and placed 1/2" higher; and the straps are: 1-1/2" X 9" each.

Hilary/T.J. 501/Christina/T.J. 512: Sleeve cuffs are 2" X 4". The skirt is 6-1/4" X 45"; and the straps are: 1-1/2" X 8-1/2" each.

Jenny/Emily: Sleeve cuffs are 2" X 4-1/4". The skirt is 6-3/4" X 45"; and the straps are: 1-1/2" X 9-1/2" each.

Angel/May/Seeley ALB9873/MB140S 14": Sleeve cuffs are 2" X 4-1/4". The skirt is 6-1/2" X 45"; and the straps are 1-1/2" X 9" each.

Elise/Georgia: Sleeve cuffs are 2" X 4-1/2". The skirt is 7-1/4" X 45"; and the straps are 1-1/2" X 9-1/2".

Shay: Sleeve cuffs are 2" X 5-1/4". The skirt is 7-1/4" X 45"; and the straps are: 1-1/2" X 9" each.

Tiffany: Sleeve cuffs are 2" X 5". The skirt is 8" X 45"; and the straps are 1-1/2" X 10" each.

Willow: Sleeve cuffs are 2" X 4-1/2". The skirt is 9" X 45"; and the straps are: 1-1/2" X 13".

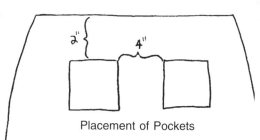

Placement of Pockets

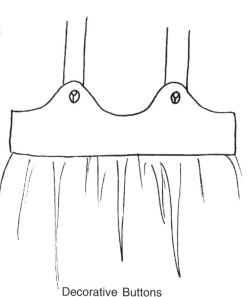

Decorative Buttons

Elise's Strawberry Yoke Dress

(Elise's body is from the pattern provided by the mold company.)

<u>Supplies:</u>

2/3 yd. strawberry print fabric
1/8 yd. contrasting fabric
1/2 yd. green baby Rick-Rack
1/3 yd. green satin ribbon, 1/8" wide
2 small snaps

BODICE

This dress has an unlined bodice. From strawberry print fabric, cut out one front and two backs, using Yoke Dress pattern pieces. Right sides together, sew front to backs at shoulder seams. Press under 1/4" the center back edges and top stitch.

To make collar, cut a piece of contrasting fabric, on grain, 1-3/4" X 15". Press under one long edge 1/4". Top stitch green Rick Rack over the folded edge. Press under the two short ends of the collar 1/4" and stitch. Run a gathering thread along the remaining unfinished edge. Wrong side of collar to right side of bodice, pull the gathering thread of the collar to fit it to the bodice neckline. Baste in place.

For neck binding, cut a bias strip from the contrasting fabric 1" X 7". Right side of bias to wrong side of bodice, and both ends of the bias strip extending beyond the center backs 1/4", sew the bias to the bodice. Press the remaining long edge of the bias under 1/4". Tucking in the short ends of the bias, fold it over to the outside of the garment and top stitch the bias to the bodice.

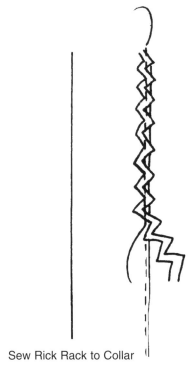

Sew Rick Rack to Collar

Cut out two sleeves from the strawberry print using Medium Sleeve pattern piece with Cuff Cutting Line. From the contrasting fabric cut two on-grain strips 2" X 4-1/2" for cuff.

Assemble sleeves according to Basic Instructions for Gathered Sleeve with Cuff. Attach sleeves to bodice and then sew underarm sleeves according to Basic Instructions.

SKIRT

Cut out a rectangle 10-3/4" X 45". Sew center back seam and hem skirt bottom as directed in Basic Instructions.

From contrasting fabric, cut out two strawberries. Right sides together, sew the two parts of the strawberry together, leaving the top open for turning. Clip curves and trim seam allowances, turn and press. Slip-stitch top opening closed. Make three loops from the green ribbon and tack it to the top of the strawberry to represent leaves. Pin the strawberry in place on the skirt, approximately 2-1/2" from the center front and 2-1/2" (should probably be less on *Shirley* and *Violet*) from the bodice/skirt seam. Top stitch around the strawberry, leaving the top open.

Gather and attach the skirt according to Basic Instructions #10. Lapping right back over left back, sew two snaps to dress bodice.

Sew Pocket to Pocket Lining

WHAT TO DO FOR OTHER DOLLS

All dolls can use the Short or Medium Sleeve pattern piece for their size, with Cuff Cutting Line.

All dolls use a 1" X 7" bias strip for the neck binding, except *Violet* (1" X 8"), *Götz/Pleasant Co.* (1" X 8-1/2") and *Tiffany* (1" X 7-1/2").

Shirley: Sleeve cuffs are 1-1/2" X 4". The skirt is 8-1/4" X 30".
Violet: Sleeve cuffs are 1-1/2" X 4-1/4". The skirt is 7-1/4" X 40".
Götz/Pleasant Co.: Sleeve cuffs are 1-1/2" X 5". The skirt is 9-1/4" X 45".
Hilary/T.J. 501/Christina/T.J. 512: Sleeve cuffs are 1-1/2" X 4". The skirt is 9-1/4" X 45".
Jenny/Emily: Sleeve cuffs are 2" X 4-1/4". The skirt is 10-1/2" X 45".
Angel/May/Seeley ALB9873/MB140S 14": Sleeve cuffs are 2" X 4-1/4". The skirt is 10-1/4" X 45".
Georgia: Use same instructions as for Elise.
Tiffany: Sleeve cuffs are 2" X 5". The skirt is 10-1/2" X 45".
Shay: Sleeve cuffs are 2" X 5-1/4". The skirt is 10-3/4" X 45".
Willow: Sleeve cuffs are 2" X 4-1/2". The skirt is 12-1/2" X 45".
Heidi: Sleeve cuffs are 2" X 5-3/4". The skirt is 11-1/4" X 45".

Top Stitch Pocket in Place

Shy Violet's Party Dress and Detached Square Collar

(Shy Violet's body is from the pattern provided by the mold company.)

<u>Supplies:</u>

1-1/4 yd. border print fabric (2/3 yd. if not a border print)
1-1/4 yd. heart-shaped, flat Cluny lace, 1" wide
2/3 yd. narrow, flat lace, 1/4" wide
1/3 yd. elastic
1/4 yd. white batiste for collar
1/2 yd. flat scalloped lace, 3/8" wide, for collar
1 yd. picot edge satin ribbon, 1/2" wide
4 small snaps

SKIRT

When working with border prints, cut out the part of the garment that requires the border first. In this case, that is the skirt, a rectangle with the long side running along the fabric's selvage, 6" X 40". Press the bottom edge of the skirt under 1/4". With the heading of the Cluny lace just underneath the folded edge of the skirt, top stitch the lace to the skirt bottom. Sew center back seam and placket as directed in Basic Instructions. Run a gathering stitch around the

top of the skirt and set it aside.

BODICE

Cut out two fronts and four backs from the non-border area of the fabric, using Waist Dress bodice pieces. Assemble bodice and bodice lining according to Basic Instructions.

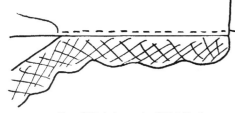

Top Stitch Lace to Skirt Bottom

Cut out two sleeves from the non-border area of the fabric, using Medium Sleeve pattern piece with Elastic Cutting Line. Attach narrow lace to bottom of sleeves according to Basic Instruction 6-a.

Assemble sleeves according to Basic Instructions for Elastic Sleeve Bottom with Ruffle. Elastic required is 6-1/2" cut in half.

Attach sleeves to bodice and then sew underarm sleeves according to Basic Instructions.

Gather and attach the skirt according to Basic Instructions #10. Lapping right back over left back, sew three snaps to dress bodice.

COLLAR

Cut out two fronts and four backs from the white batiste, using Detached Square Collar pattern pieces. Right sides together, sew one front to two backs to make collar. Repeat with remaining pieces for collar lining.

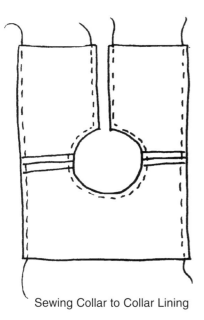

Sewing Collar to Collar Lining

Right sides together, sew collar to collar lining by stitching along center backs, around neckline and on sides. Leave bottom edges of collar front and backs open for turning. Clip curves, trim seam allowances and turn right side out. Press.

Right sides up, place scalloped lace on bottom edges of collar front and backs, so that all of the lace is actually on fabric. Zig-zag with a tight stitch around the scallops. With a small, sharp scissors, trim away most of the collar fabric underneath the lace. Use Fray-Chek on the ends of the lace to keep it from fraying.

Cut out a flower motif from the border print fabric. Use Fray-Chek around all the edges and glue or hand stitch flower to lower left front of collar. If you want to try a bit of applique stitch, this is a nice small project to learn on. Using one strand of matching embroidery floss, work a blanket stitch as shown around the motif. Or, you can always try a little puff paint of paint embroidery without the fabric motif at all. Ribbon roses? Purchased appliques? Use a companion print fabric instead of white for the collar? Go for it! Incidentally, this style dress really lends itself to holiday prints and all the companion trims.

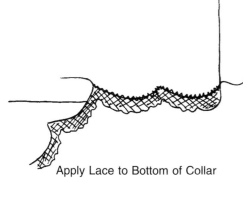

Apply Lace to Bottom of Collar

The hat we show in our teatime scene was purchased from the craft department of a dime store. We cut the picot edge ribbon in half and tied one piece around the hat and the other around the doll's waist for a belt.

WHAT TO DO FOR OTHER DOLLS

Shirley: Skirt is 6" X 30". Sleeve elastic is 3-1/2" each.

Götz/Pleasant Co.: The skirt is 7-1/4" X 40". Sleeve elastic is 4-1/4" each.
Hilary/T.J. 501/Christina/T.J. 512: The skirt is 7-1/4" X 45". Sleeve elastic is 3-1/2" each.
Jenny/Emily: The skirt is 7-3/4" X 45". Sleeve elastic is 3-3/4" each.
Angel/May/Seeley ALB9873/MB140S 14": The skirt is 7-1/2" X 45". Sleeve elastic is 3-3/4" each.
Elise/Georgia: The skirt is 8-1/4" X 45". Sleeve elastic is 3-1/2" each.
Shay: The skirt is 8-1/4" X 45". Sleeve elastic is 4" each.
Tiffany: The skirt is 8-3/4" X 45". Sleeve elastic is 4-1/4" each.
Willow: The skirt is 9-3/4" X 45". Sleeve elastic is 3-1/4" each.
Heidi: The skirt is 8-1/4" X 45". Sleeve elastic is 5" each.

Christina's Candy Stripe Dress and Scalloped Pinafore

(Christina's body is the all porcelain T.J. 512.)

Supplies:

2/3 yd. pink and white striped taffeta
1/2 yd. Swiss batiste for pinafore
4 yd. flat cotton lace, 1" wide, for Christina (others see below)
2-1/3 yd. entredeux
pink and green embroidery floss
6 small snaps

BODICE

Cut out two fronts and four backs from striped taffeta fabric, using Waist Dress bodice pieces. Assemble bodice and bodice lining according to Basic Instructions.

Cut out two sleeves, using Short Sleeve pattern piece with Cuff Cutting Line and two bias strips 1" X 4" for sleeve binding.

Assemble sleeves according to Basic Instructions for Puffed Sleeve with Narrow Binding.

Attach sleeves to bodice and then sew underarm sleeves according to Basic Instructions.

SKIRT

Cut a rectangle 8-1/4" X 45". Sew center back seam and hem skirt bottom as directed in Basic Instructions.

Gather and attach the skirt according to Basic Instructions #10. Lapping right back over left back, sew three snaps to dress bodice.

SCALLOPED PINAFORE

Embroidery Design
for Pinafore Bib

**Sew Bib to Bib Lining
Across the Top Only**

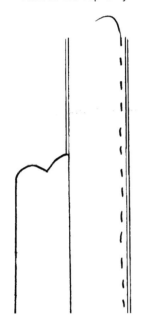

Sew Strap to Side of Bib

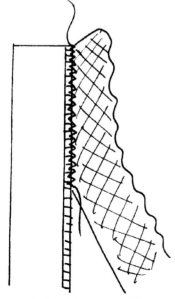

**Zig-zag Lace to Entredeux
on Strap**

Trace two bib fronts from Scalloped Pinafore pattern piece onto Swiss batiste, but do not cut out yet. For the pinafore skirt, draw a 6-1/4" X 40" rectangle on the batiste, but do not cut it out yet. Trace the Scallop 10 times along one long side of the rectangle. Trace the bullion rosebud in each scallop and the nosegay of bullion rosebuds onto one of the bib fronts. Using a small embroidery hoop, a #7-8 embroidery needle and two strands of floss, work the flowers as shown. When all embroidery is finished, press it right side down on a clean towel. Then cut out the bibs and pinafore skirt.

Right sides together, sew the bib to the bib lining across the scalloped top only, leaving the sides and bottom unstitched. Clip curves and trim seam allowances. Turn right side out and press.

Cut out four straps 2-1/2" X 11". Sew a strap to each side of the bib front by sandwiching the bib between two straps as shown. Stitch along the bib side of one long edge of the straps. Turn the straps right side out and press.

Cut two pieces of entredeux the same length as the straps. Trim away almost all of the excess fabric on one side of the entredeux. Treating both layers of the strap as one unit, and right sides together, zig-zag the entredeux to the unfinished side of each strap, keeping the strap exposed 1/8" of an inch beyond the entredeux. This extension will curl right into the zig-zagging and make a clean finish. See Basic Instructions for French Machine Sewing, Lace-to-Fabric technique.

Cut two pieces of lace each double the length of the straps. Pull the gathering thread so that the lace fits the strap. Right sides up and entredeux flush with lace heading, zig-zag lace to entredeux.

Trim away most of the excess fabric from one edge of the remaining entredeux. Right sides together, pin the entredeux to the pinafore skirt along the scallops, mitering corners. See Basic Instructions for French Machine Sewing, Lace-to-Fabric technique. Zig-zag the entredeux in place and press. Pull the gathering thread of the remaining lace and spread it out evenly along the scallops. Right sides up, zig-zag the lace to the entredeux.

Narrow hem the center backs (short ends of the rectangle) of the pinafore skirt. Run a gathering thread along the top of the pinafore skirt. Cut out a waistband on grain, 1-1/2" X 11". Right side of waistband to wrong side of pinafore skirt, and ends of waistband extending 1/4" beyond center backs of skirt, sew waistband to pinafore. Press the remaining long edge of the waistband 1/4" toward the wrong side. Tucking in the ends, fold the waistband to the outside of the garment and top stitch in place.

Center the bib on the skirt with the bottom of the bib extending approximately 1/4" beyond the bottom edge of the waistband, and top stitch it in place.

Try the pinafore on the doll and mark where the waistband snap should go, lapping right back over left. Cross the straps in back and mark where you want the snaps on the straps. The snaps should end up 1" on either side of the center back.

WHAT TO DO FOR OTHER DOLLS

All dolls can use the Short or Medium Sleeve pattern piece for their size, with Cuff Cutting Line. (Pinafore straps are of generous length so they can be crossed in back.)

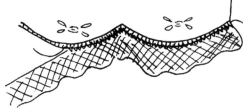

Attaching Lace to Entredeux
on Bottom of Pinafore

Shirley: Requires 3-1/4 yd. lace. Skirt is 7" X 32". Sleeve bindings are 1" x 4". The pinafore skirt is 5" X 32"; the straps are 1-1/4" X 9" each; the waistband is 1-1/2" X 10".

Violet: Requires 3-7/8 yd. lace. The skirt is 7-1/2" X 40". Sleeve bindings are 1" X 4-1/4". The pinafore skirt is 5-1/2" X 40"; the straps are 1-1/4" X 9" each; the waistband is 1-1/2" X 11".

Götz/Pleasant Co.: Requires 4 yd. lace. The skirt is 8-1/4" X 40". Sleeve bindings are 1 X 5". The pinafore skirt is 6-1/4" X 40"; the straps are 1-1/4" X 11" each; the waistband is 1-1/2" X 12".

Hilary/T.J. 501: Follow Christina's instructions exactly.

Jenny/Emily: Requires 4-1/2 yd. lace. The skirt is 8-3/4" X 45". Sleeve bindings are 1" X 4-1/4". The pinafore skirt is 6-3/4" X 44"; the straps are 1-1/4" X 11-1/2" each; the waistband is 2" X 13-1/4".

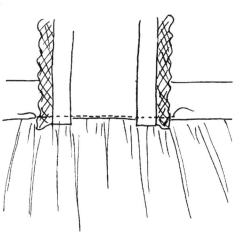

Top Stitch Straps and
Bib to Pinafore Skirt

Angel/May/Seeley ALB9873/MB140S 14": Requires 4-1/4 yd. lace. The skirt is 8-1/2" X 45". Sleeve bindings are 1" X 4-1/4". The pinafore skirt is 6-1/2" X 44"; the straps are 1-1/4" X 11" each; the waistband is 2" X 11".

Elise/Georgia: Requires 4-1/2 yd. lace. The skirt is 9-1/4" X 45". Sleeve bindings are 1" X 4-1/2". The pinafore skirt is 7-1/4" X 44"; the straps are 1-1/4" X 11-1/2" each; the waistband is 2" X 12".

Shay: Requires 4-1/3 yd. lace. The skirt is 9-1/4" X 45". Sleeve bindings are 1" X 5-1/4". The pinafore skirt is 7-1/4" X 44"; the straps are 1-1/4" X 11" each; the waistband is 2" X 11-1/4".

Tiffany: Requires 4-1/2 yd. lace. The skirt is 9-3/4" X 45". Sleeve bindings are 1" X 5". The pinafore skirt is 7-3/4" X 44"; the straps are 1-1/4" X 12" each; the waistband is 2" X 11-1/2".

Willow: Requires 4-3/4 yd. lace. The skirt is 10-3/4" X 45". Sleeve bindings are 1" X 4-1/2". The pinafore skirt is 8-3/4" X 44"; the straps are 1-1/4" X 15" each; the waistband is 2" X 12-3/4".

Heidi: Requires 4-1/2 yd. lace. The skirt is 9-1/4" X 45". Sleeve bindings are 1" X 5-3/4". The pinafore skirt is 7-1/4" X 44"; the straps are 1-1/4" X 13"; the waistband is 2" X 14-3/4".

Elise's Smocked Frock and Floppy Hat

(Elise's body is from the pattern provided by the mold company.)

Supplies:

2/3 yd. floral fabric
15" flat lace, 1-1/2" wide, for collar
2/3 yd. flat, narrow lace, 3/8" wide
1/4 yd. baby piping or cord and bias fabric to make piping
embroidery floss
3 small snaps
1/3 yd. fabric for hat
1/4 yd. medium weight interfacing for hat
48" flat, medium lace, 1" wide, for hat

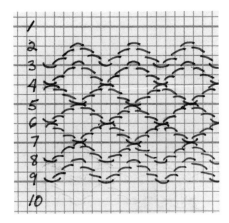

Scrap of 1/4" wide ribbon for hat bow

BODICE

Cut out two fronts and four backs using Yoke Dress bodice pieces. Assemble bodice and bodice lining according to Basic Instructions. Right sides together, sew bodice to bodice lining along center backs only. Turn right side out and press.

To make collar, gather the 1-1/2" wide lace to fit around the neckline. Wrong side of lace to right side of bodice, with short ends of the lace folded under 1/4", baste the lace to the neck edge, treating bodice and bodice lining as one unit.

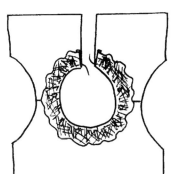

Sew Gathered Collar
to Neckline

Cut a bias strip from the floral fabric 1" X 7". Right side of bias to wrong side of bodice, and both ends of the bias strip extending beyond the center backs 1/4", sew the bias to the bodice. Press the remaining long edge of the bias under 1/4". Tucking in the short ends of the bias, fold it over to the outside of the garment and top stitch the bias to the bodice.

Cut out two sleeves using Medium Sleeve pattern piece with Elastic Cutting Line. Attach narrow lace to bottom of sleeves according to Basic Instruction 6-a.

Assemble sleeves according to Basic Instructions for Elastic Sleeve Bottom with Ruffle. Elastic required is 7" cut in half.

Attach sleeves to bodice and then sew underarm sleeves according to Basic Instructions.

SMOCKED SKIRT

Cut a rectangle of fabric 10-3/4" X 45". Fold it in half cross-wise so you have a rectangle 10-3/4" X 22-1/2". Cut the fabric in half along the fold line. Now you have a front and a back skirt.

Enclose Neckline of
Collar in Bias Binding

Fold the back skirt in half so that you have a rectangle 10-3/4" X 11-1/4". Cut the fabric in half along the fold line. Now you have a left back and a right back skirt. Sew center back seam and finish placket as directed in Basic Instructions, #8, but do not hem. Gather the tops of the skirt backs and set aside.

Starting 1/4" in from top edge of skirt front, pleat it with 10 half-space rows. Pull the gathering threads so that the skirt front is 6-3/4" wide. Smock according to smocking graph, beginning on row 2 of the pleating. When smocking is completed, remove all pleating threads except the top one.

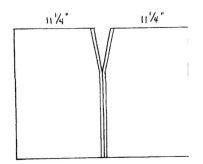

Center Back of Skirt

Pin piping to top of skirt front, right sides together, so that the stitching line of the piping runs along the top pleating thread. Stitch, following the top pleating thread.

Right sides together, sew smocked skirt front to skirt backs at side seams. To hem, turn up bottom of skirt 1/4" and press. Turn up another 1" and stitch.

Pull gathering threads of skirt backs so that when you pin the bodice to the skirt, right sides together, they match. Stitch. Lapping right back over left back, sew three snaps to dress bodice.

HAT

This hat fits all of the dolls shown in the book, although fullness of wigs can make it fit differently. If you really need to re-size the hat for a completely different size doll, try reducing or enlarging the pattern pieces on a photocopy machine. (Yes, we gladly give you permission to photocopy parts of our book for your own personal use.)

There are three parts to this hat, besides the bow. They are: the crown, which is the top part; the rise, which is the part that connects the crown and the brim; and the brim.

Cut out one crown from the fabric and one from the interfacing. The rise is a rectangle 1-3/4" X 12-1/2", one cut from fabric and one cut from interfacing. Cut two brims from the fabric and one from the interfacing, using the Lace Trimmed Hat cutting line.

Baste interfacing to wrong side of rise, crown and one brim.

Gather the 48" of 1" wide lace so that it fits around the outside edge of the brim. Pin it, right side down, to the interfaced brim. This is similar to sewing a ruffle on a pillow. Baste the lace in place.

Right sides together, sew the remaining brim to the interfaced brim, stitching only around the outside circle. Clip and trim seam allowances, turn right side out and press. Baste all three layers together by stitching around the inner circle.

Make a circle of the interfaced rise by sewing the short ends together (right sides together, of course). Right sides together, sew the rise to the crown. Clip curves and trim seam allowances. Similarly, sew the brim to the rise.

Cut a rectangle of the floral fabric 2" X 9". Fold the ends under so that you get a piece 1-1/2" X 3-1/2". Wrap the scrap of ribbon around it, hand stitch to secure the "bow." Bend the front of the brim up to the rise, tack it and the bow in place.

WHAT TO DO FOR OTHER DOLLS

All dolls can use the Short or Medium Sleeve pattern piece for their size, with Elastic Cutting Line.

Shirley: Skirt is 8-1/4" X 30". Sleeve elastic is 3-1/2" each.
Violet: Skirt is 7-1/4" X 40". Sleeve elastic is 3-1/4" each.
Götz/Pleasant Co.: The skirt is 9-1/4" X 40". Sleeve elastic is 4-1/4" each.
Hilary/T.J. 501/Christina/T.J. 512: The skirt is 9-1/4" X 45". Sleeve elastic is 3-1/2" each.
Jenny/Emily: The skirt is 10-1/2" X 45". Sleeve elastic is 3-3/4" each.
Angel/May/Seeley ALB9873/MB140S 14": The skirt is 10-1/4" X 45". Sleeve elastic is 3-3/4" each.

76

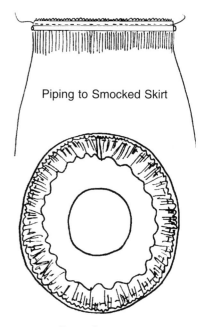

Piping to Smocked Skirt

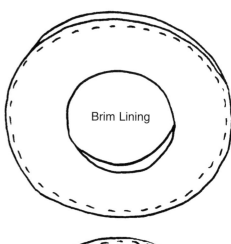

Baste Lace to
Interfaced Brim

Brim Lining

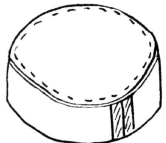

Rise and Crown of Hat

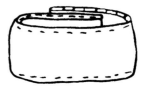

Hemmed Fabric
Forms Bow

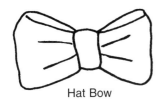

Hat Bow

Georgia: The skirt is 10-3/4" X 45". Sleeve elastic is 3-1/2" each.
Shay: The skirt is 10-3/4" X 45". Sleeve elastic is 4" each.
Tiffany: The skirt is 10-1/2" X 45". Sleeve elastic is 4-1/4" each.
Willow: The skirt is 12-1/2" X 45". Sleeve elastic is 3-1/4" each.
Heidi: The skirt is 11-1/4" X 45". Sleeve elastic is 5" each.

Angel's French Heirloom Dress and Hat

(Angel's body is from Seeley's porcelain ALB9873 mold.)

Supplies:

2/3 yd. cotton Swiss batiste
2-3/4 yd. narrow entredeux
1/3 yd. wide entredeux (or 1/3 yd. more narrow entredeux)
1/3 yd. narrow lace edging (1/4"-3/8")
3-1/4 yd. wide insertion (1/2")
1-2/3 yd. narrow insertion (3/8")
5-3/4 yd. wide lace edging (1") (For Shirley and Violet, see below)
1-1/4 yd. narrow satin ribbon (1/4") for hat
1/2 yd. white cloth-covered wire for hat
2 small snaps

Sewing this dress is no different than sewing any other yoke dress, except that something called entredeux has been substituted for sleeve elastic or cuff, and something called lace insertion has been substituted for fabric in various locations for the purpose of "fancying up" a cotton dress. See Basic Instructions for specific techniques.

BODICE

Cut out one front and two backs from Yoke Dress bodice pattern pieces. Cut out two sleeves using Short Sleeve pattern with Cuff Cutting Line.

Karen's First Communion

Measure a piece of narrow lace insertion the same height as the center of the front yoke plus 3/4". Cut two pieces of medium insertion the same length. Using Lace-to-Lace Technique, make a fancy band by sewing the wider lace insertion to both sides of the narrow lace insertion as shown in the Basic Instructions for French Machine Sewing.

Right sides up, center this fancy band vertically on the yoke front. Zig-zag along the two outside edges of the wider insertion pieces. With a small, sharp scissors, carefully cut away the fabric behind the insertion. Press.

Right sides together, sew the front and back yokes together at the shoulders. Narrow hem the center back edges.

Bodice Fancy Band

Using Entredeux-to-Flat-Fabric French Machine Sewing Technique in Basic Instructions, sew narrow entredeux to the neckline. Gather the narrow lace edging to fit the neckline and zig-zag in place, using Gathered Lace-to-Entredeux French Machine Sewing Technique, being sure to fold the short ends of the lace under 1/4".

SLEEVES

Gather the lower edge of both sleeves. Using Entredeux-to-Gathered-Fabric French Machine Sewing Technique, apply 4-1/2" wide entredeux to each sleeve bottom. Gather 8-1/2" of the wide lace edging for each sleeve and apply it to the wide entredeux, using Gathered Lace-to-Entredeux French Machine Sewing Technique.

Gather sleeve caps to fit bodice armholes. Right sides together, sew sleeves to bodice and sew underarm seams as directed in Basic Instructions.

SKIRT

Cut out a skirt 7-1/2" X 45".

Make a fancy band to go around the skirt as follows, using the various French Machine Sewing Techniques described above. Sew a 45" length of wider lace insertion to both sides of a 45" length of narrower lace insertion. Apply 45" of narrow entredeux to one side of this band. Gather 90" of wide lace edging and apply it to the other side of the band. Now sew the entredeux side to the bottom of the skirt.

Carefully matching the seams of all the lace components, sew the center back seam of the skirt, leaving approximately the top 3" open. Finish off the opening as directed in the Basic Instructions by narrow hemming and stitching around it.

Gather the skirt to fit the bodice. Right sides together, stitch. Trim away excess seam allowance fabric.

BODICE RUFFLE

Cut a piece of narrow entredeux long enough to go around the front bodice, over the shoulders and across the back bodices as shown. Cut a piece of wide lace double the length of the entredeux you just cut. Gather the lace to fit the entredeux. Trim away one edge of the fabric from the entredeux and zig-zag the gathered lace edging to it, turning under the short ends of the lace 1/4". Trim away the remaining fabric from the entredeux.

Pin the lace/entredeux trim around the bodice as shown in the diagram so that it frames the bodice. Zig-zag in place.

Lapping right center back over left, sew snaps to center back.

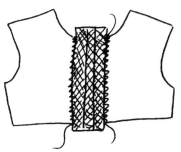

Sewing Fancy Band
to Bodice

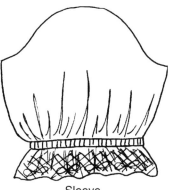

Sleeve

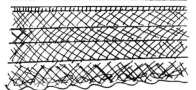

Skirt Fancy Band

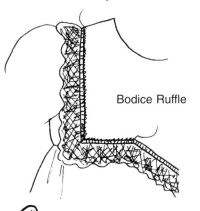

Bodice Ruffle

Bodice Ruffle,
Back View

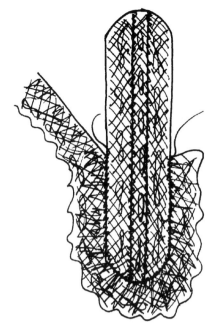

Hat Construction

Loops of Ribbon for Fru-Fru

Completed Fru-Fru

HAT

All the dolls featured in this book can wear the same hat.

Cut two pieces of wide lace insertion 7" long and one piece of narrower lace insertion 7" long. Using lace-to-lace French machine technique, sew them together with the narrower insertion in the middle. Trim the corners of the resulting rectangle so that they are rounded.

Gather one yard of the 1" wide lace edging so that it fits around the hat. Right sides up, zig-zag it to the perimeter of the hat.

Bend the wire so that it fits around the insertion part of the hat. Zig-zag it to the wrong side of the hat, trying not to catch the lace edging in the stitching. To make "fru-frus", cut the narrow ribbon in half. Make several loops and tack them together, then tack to the lower edge of each side of the hat. Bend the hat to fit the doll's head.

NOTE: You can turn this into a First Communion ensemble by attaching a rectangle of white netting to the back of the hat for a veil.

WHAT TO DO FOR OTHER DOLLS

All dolls can use the Short or Medium Sleeve pattern piece for their size, with Cuff Cutting Line.

Shirley: Needs only 4-1/2 yd. wide lace edging. 4" wide entredeux and 8" wide lace per sleeve. The skirt is 5-3/4" X 36". The skirt's fancy band is 30" long, not 45".
Violet: Needs only 4-3/4 yd. wide lace edging. 4-1/4" wide entredeux and 8-1/2" lace per sleeve. The skirt is 4-3/4" X 40". The skirt's fancy band is 40" long, not 45".
Götz/Pleasant Co.: 5" wide entredeux and 10" wide lace edging per sleeve. The skirt is 9-1/4" X 45".
Hilary/T.J. 501/Christina/T.J. 512: 4" entredeux and 8" lace per sleeve. The skirt is 6-3/4" X 45".
Jenny/Emily: 4-1/4" entredeux and 8-1/12" lace per sleeve. The skirt is 8" X 45".
May/MB140S 14": Follow instructions for Angel.
Elise/Georgia: 4-1/2" entredeux and 9" lace per sleeve. The skirt is 8-1/4" X 45".
Tiffany: 5" entredeux and 10" lace per sleeve. The skirt is 8" X 45".
Shay: 5-1/4" entredeux and 10-1/2" lace per sleeve. The skirt is 8-1/4" X 45".
Willow: 4-1/2" entredeux and 9" lace per sleeve. The skirt is 10" X 45".
Heidi: 5-3/4" entredeux and 11-1/2" lace per sleeve. The skirt is 8-3/4" X 45".

Suppliers of Molds, Bodies, Wigs, Shoes and Accessories

(Call or write for catalogs. Some companies charge for their catalogs.)

Bell Ceramics, Inc.
P.O. Box 120127
Clermont, FL 34712
1-800-874-9025

Doll Artworks, The
12623 Perimeter Drive
Dallas, TX 75228
1-214-270-8095

Doll Carriage, The
6405 Encantado Court
Rockford, MI 49341
1-616-874-6111

Dollspart Supply Co., Inc.
8000 Cooper Ave., Bldg. #28
Glendale, NY 11385
1-718-326-4500

Expressions
P.O. Box 174
Jamestown, MO 65046
1-800-452-2480

Global Dolls Corp.
1903 Aviation Blvd.
Lincoln, CA 95648
1-800-GLOBAL-7

Götz Dolls, Inc.
8257 Loop Road--Radisson
Baldwinsville, NY 13027
1-315-635-1055

Klowns by Kay
2632 Lakehill
Carrollton, TX 75006
1-214-418-0909

LaSioux
75 Arkansas Street
San Francisco, CA 94107
1-415-431-7122

Monique Trading Corporation
1369 Rollins Road
Burlingame, CA 94010
1-800-621-4338

Playhouse Import/Export, Inc.
15377 Huntwood Avenue
Hayward, CA 94544
1-510-785-1352

Pleasant Company
8400 Fairway Place
P.O. Box 620190
Middleton, WI 53562-0190
1-800-845-0005

Scioto Doll Mold Co.
Division of Powers Ceramic Supply
2208 East 6th Street
Tulsa, OK 74104
1-918-592-2808

Seeley's
P.O. Box 669
Oneonta, NY 13820
1-607-433-1240

Tallina's Doll Supplies, Inc.
15790 SE Highway 224
Clackamas, OR 97015
1-503-658-6148

Ultimate Collection, Inc., The
12773 West Forest Hill Blvd., #1208
West Palm Beach, FL 33414
1-407-790-0137

Wee Three, Inc.
130 Doolittle Drive, Unit #4
San Leandro, CA 94577
1-510-632-1101